ECCLESIASTES

Readings: A New Biblical Commentary

ECCLESIASTES

Barbara M. Leung Lai

SHEFFIELD PHOENIX PRESS
2024

Copyright © 2024 Sheffield Phoenix Press
Published by Sheffield Phoenix Press
University of Sheffield, S10 2TN

www.sheffieldphoenix.com

All rights reserved.
No part of this publication may be reproduced or transmitted in any form or by any means, electronic or mechanical, including photocopying, recording or any information storage or retrieval system, without the publisher's permission in writing.

A CIP catalogue record for this book
is available from the British Library

Typeset by the HK Scriptorium

ISBN: 978-1-914490-84-4 (HB)
ISBN: 978-1-914490-49-1 (PB)

*In Memory of my Fellow Pilgrims—
those who had fought the good fight,
those who had finished the race,
and had kept the faith.
(2 Timothy 4.7)*

Contents

Preface and Acknowledgements   xi

Abbreviations   xiii

Introduction   1
   The Book   1
   Authorship and Dating   2
   Ecclesiastes as Wisdom Literature   4
   Message   5

Approaching Ecclesiastes: Reading Strategies   7
   Reading Narrativally   7
   Reading Polyphonically   8
   Reading Dialectically   10
   Reading 'Cross the Grains'   11
   Reading as a 'Memoir'   12

Text and Analysis of Speaking Voices   16

Commentary   35
A. Third-Person Frame Narrator Introducing Qohelet and the Fundamental Conviction: 'Vanity of vanities! All Is Vanity!' (1.1-3)   40

B. Second-Person Collective Voice of Wisdom Spelling Out the Conviction of God's Order of Creation and the Order of God's Ruling (1.4-11)   41

C. Qohelet's First-Person Voice Reflecting on his *Personal Life Experience* (in Dialogue with his Inner Voice) (1.12–2.26)   44
   1. First personal experience (1.12-18)   44
      Reflective summary: 'And behold, all is vanity, a chasing after the wind!' (1.14)
      'This too, is a chasing after the wind!' (1.17)   44
   2. Second personal experience (2.1-11)   46

		Reflective summary: 'And behold, this also is vanity!' (2.1)	
		'And behold, all was vanity and a chasing after the wind!' (2.11)	46
	3.	Third personal experience (2.12-23)	47
		Reflective summary: 'All is vanity, a chasing after the wind!' (2.17)	
		'This too is vanity!' (2.23)	47
	4.	First *carpe diem* saying (2.24-26)	50
		Reflective summary: 'This too is vanity, a chasing after the wind!' (2.26)	50
D.	Second-Person Voice of Wisdom Affirming God's Order of Things (3.1-15)		52
	1.	There is a time for everything (3.1-11)	52
	2.	Second *carpe diem* saying (3.12-13) and the ending (3.14-15)	54
E.	Qohelet's First-Person Voice Reflecting on his *Exploration of Life* in Dialogue with his Inner Voice (3.16-4.16)		55
	1.	First cycle of exploration (3.16-21)	55
	2.	Third *carpe diem* saying (3.22)	57
	3.	Second cycle of exploration (4.1-3)	57
	4.	Third cycle of exploration (4.4)	58
		Interlude: Second-person wisdom sayings (4.5-6)	58
	5.	Fourth cycle of exploration (4.7-16)	59
		Interlude: Second-person wisdom sayings (4.9-14)	59
		Reflective summary: 'This too is vanity, a chasing after the wind!' (4.15-16)	60
F.	Second-Person Wisdom's Instruction on 'Fearing God' (5.1-7 [MT 4.17–5.6])		61
		Interlude: Second-person wisdom sayings (5.8-12 [MT 5.7-11])	63
G.	Qohelet's First-Person *Exploration of Life* Continued (5.13–6.12 [MT 5.12–6.12])		64
	1.	Fifth cycle of exploration (5.13-17 [MT 5.12-16])	64
	2.	Fourth *carpe diem* saying (5.18-20 [MT 5.17-19])	66
	3.	Sixth cycle of exploration (6.1-12)	67
H.	Second-Person Wisdom Sayings (7.1-14)		70
	1.	'Better than' sayings (7.1-12)	70
	2.	Wisdom's voice affirming the order of God's ruling (7.12-13)	74
I.	Qohelet's First-Person *Exploration of Life* Continued (7.15–10.7)		74
	1.	Seventh cycle of exploration (7.15-18)	74
		Interlude: Second-person wisdom sayings (7.19-22)	77

	2. Eighth cycle of exploration (7.23-26)	77
	3. Ninth cycle of exploration (7.27–8.8)	79
	Interlude: Second-person wisdom sayings (8.1-8)	80
	4. Tenth cycle of exploration (8.9-13)	82
	Reflective summary: on fearing God (8.12-13)	83
	5. Eleventh cycle of exploration (8.14)	83
	6. Fifth *carpe diem* saying (8.15)	84
	7. Twelfth cycle of exploration (8.16-17)	85
	8. Thirteenth cycle of exploration (9.1-2)	85
	9. Fourteenth cycle of exploration (9.3-6)	87
	10. Sixth *carpe diem* saying (9.7-10)	89
	11. Fifteenth cycle of exploration (9.11-12)	91
	12. Sixteenth cycle of exploration (9.13-16)	92
	Interlude: Second-person wisdom sayings	
	Wisdom is indeed better than folly (9.17–10.4)	93
	13. Seventeenth cycle of exploration (10.5-7)	94
J.	Second-Person Wisdom Sayings (10.8-12.7)	95
	1. Wisdom is indeed better than folly: The strength and limits of wisdom (10.8-20)	96
	2. Advice for life in view of the uncertainties of the risky future (11.1-8)	98
	3. Seventh *carpe diem* saying (11.9-10)	101
	4. Live life fully in the 'present' and aware of the certainty of bad times: 'Remember your Creator!' (12.1-7)	102
K.	Qohelet's First-Person Summary Appraisal, Echoing the Fundamental Conviction: 'Vanity of vanities! All Is Vanity!' (12.8)	105
L.	Voice of the Epilogist Responding to Qohelet's Fundamental Conviction about Life: 'Vanity of Vanities! All Is Vanity!' (12.9-14)	106

Conclusion	108
Select Bibliography	110
Index of References	115
Index of Authors	120

Preface and Acknowledgments

Life itself is complex and enigmatic. For some, embracing coexisting polar tensions seems to be part of life's challenge. I am writing this preface while cruising the Mediterranean at the beginning of the Israel–Hamas war. The tragic loss of more than five hundred innocent lives due to the hospital blast and its aftermath have saddened my heart enormously. To say the least, I am disturbed by what is happening in Israel and Gaza and elsewhere in the world. Hatred, revenge, the loss of human dignity and the right to survive—all these have shaken our worldview to its core and provoke us to rethink what it means to be human. Yet, at the same time, I am doing the things that an average cruise passenger would do—eat, drink and be merry; doing things you would not normally do in real life: no-guilt three desserts a day; dancing with the crowd till midnight; and keep reminding myself that 'I am on vacation'. After all, we are encouraged to do exactly what Qohelet is urging us to do—'This is what I have observed to be good: that it is appropriate for a person to eat, to drink and find satisfaction in their toilsome labor under the sun during the few days of life God has given them—for this is their lot' (5.18 [MT 17]). Certainly, this is our 'lot', a gift from God; and there is a time for everything—'a time to mourn and a time to dance; a time for war and a time for peace' (3.4b, 8b). However, we do wish life were that simple—in that time and season are marked with clear boundaries with no overlapping or blurring transitions. I believe Eccl. 3.4, 8; 5.18 [MT 17] are truths, but in no way can they represent the *whole* truth of humanity's collective lived experience under the sun. Qohelet ponders the meaning of life self-engagingly and finds it utterly absurd! He struggles and is greatly distressed. And so am I.

As an ancient text on life experience and exploration of life and its meaning, Ecclesiastes does speak profoundly to us today. It provides the flesh-and-blood slices of reality that we all face at different seasons of our lives. I am immensely motivated to journey with my audience to dive in its immersed paradoxes and resurface with a more balanced view of its core message about how to live. My lifelong love for wisdom literature has been significantly deepened with this endeavour—writing a commentary for first-time readers of Ecclesiastes.

It has been my desire to write a book for a commemorative purpose after my retirement from full-time teaching. Personally, I find it very fitting to dedicate this commentary in memory of my dear friends—the cloud of witnesses whose lives have powerfully imparted to me the wisdom about the hows of embracing life with all its realities.

I am grateful to Jeremy Clines of Sheffield Phoenix Press for accepting to publish my book for the Readings Series. Tyndale students of my advanced Bible elective class on Ecclesiastes had contributed their significant efforts in test-reading the book dialogically through voice analysis. The Leung sisters and members of my cell group have been a constant support for this project, particularly when I faced my own challenging times. On top of a demanding job and as the parent of two young children, I have been assisted by my son Eusebius, who has graciously devoted his time in proofreading the drafts. Warren, the love of my life, has passionately stood by me. For his interest and active participation in my writings, and always lending an ear to listen to my 'ah-ha!' moments, I offer my deep appreciation.

Barbara M. Leung Lai
Canadian Thanksgiving, October 2023

Abbreviations

AB	Anchor Bible
BCOTWP	Baker Commentary of the Old Testament: Wisdom and Psalms
Bib	*Biblica*
BBR	*Bulletin for Biblical Research*
CBQ	*Catholic Biblical Quarterly*
FQS	*Forum: Qualitative Social Research*
GBS	Guides to Biblical Scholarship
HBM	Hebrew Bible Monographs
HBT	*Horizon in Biblical Theology*
ICC	International Critical Commentary
IVP	InterVarsity Press
JBL	*Journal for the Studies of Biblical Literature*
JR	*Journal of Religion*
JSOT	*Journal for the Study of the Old Testament*
JSOTSup	Journal for the Study of the Old Testament, Supplement Series
NCB	New Century Bible
NICOT	New International Commentary of the Old Testament
NIV	New International Version
OTE	*Old Testament Essays*
OTL	Old Testament Library
TOTC	Tyndale Old Testament Commentaries
TynB	Tyndale Bulletin
WBC	Word Biblical Commentary

Introduction

A. The Book

Ecclesiastes is a strange book. To the interested, engaged reader, the book gives the general impression of being elusive, perplexing, contradictory and pessimistic. Five observations may emerge after a close reading of the chapters. *First*, there are conflicting ideologies as compared to the rest of the Old Testament, primarily with a focus on the so-called two-way doctrine (or the blessing-and-cursing principle after Ps. 1.1-4; cf. Deut. 11.26-28; 28.1, 15; Prov. 3.33 vs., e.g., 7.15; 8.14-15; 9.1-6). *Second*, in the captivating 'I'-voice of Qohelet/the preacher (hereafter, 'Qohelet' refers to the person behind the 'I'-voice), there is a multiplicity of speaking voices that creates both the dialogic and dialectic dynamics in the book. *Third*, the deeply reflective and yet thinking-out-loud mode of expression of Qohelet gives the notion of the lack of any logical or structural development through the twelve chapters. *Fourth*, while the pessimistic summary appraisal—'Vanity of vanities! All is vanity/a chasing after the wind!' (e.g. 1.2, 14; 2.1, 26; 4.16; 12.8)—pronounced by Qohelet's enticing 'I'-voice is dominant, seven uplifting and kerygmatic *carpe diem* (i.e. 'seize the day') short sayings appear sparingly throughout the book (2.24-25; 3.12-13; 3.22; 5.18-20 [MT 17-19]; 8.15; 9.7-10; 11.9-10). *Fifth*, the epilogist's abrupt closing remarks in 12.9-14 (esp. after Qohelet's outcry in 12.8) breaks the dialogic and dialectic thrust of one's reading, leaving the notion of a sudden, top-down and dogmatic concluding statement—most unsatisfying and, to a certain extent, troubling to the reader. These five textual observations would serve as the impetus inviting us to engage in unpacking the complexity of this highly ambiguous and yet intriguing book.

Ecclesiastes is also a polyphony (see discussion in 'Text and Analysis of Speaking Voices'). With the focus of scholarly attention on voice analysis in the past decade (see Greenwood 2012; Leung Lai 2013, 2021), a total of five voices have been identified: (1) the first-person 'I'-voice of Qohelet (e.g. 1.1-2a; 1.12-14); (2) Qohelet's own inner voice (e.g. 1.16; 2.1-2; 3.17-18); (3) the third-person voice of the frame narrator (1.1-2a; 7.27; 12.8); (4) the second-person collective voice of wisdom (e.g. 4.9-13; 5.1-7

[MT 4.17–5.6]); and (5) the voice of the epilogist (12.9-14). These five, sometimes contending voices engage in vibrant dialogues with one other. Through these vigorous and lively interactions, an additional window of perception is provided for us (as compared to a single-voice book; see discussion in 'Approaching Ecclesiastes: Reading Strategies' section, esp. on the Bakhtinian 'dialogic truth').

Identification of the book's dominant genre(s) and the employment of fitting reading strategies are interrelated. There is no single genre that can be assigned to Ecclesiastes. It combines elements known to wisdom literature: reflection, autobiography, proverbial saying, counsel/instruction and poetry (see Fox 1999: 153). Efforts in fine-tuning the identification and analysis of the literary genres represented have yielded impactful results toward the reading strategy and thus interpretation of the book. Among the more recent commentators, Knut Heim's reading of the book as 'resistant literature in the form of political satire' (see Heim 2019: 4-5; Jarick 2014: 177) and reading as 'a memoir of Qohelet' with therapeutic effect upon the memoirist as advocated in the present commentary (see esp. the discussion in 'Reading as a Memoir'; cf. Fox's view of the book as a report of a journey of consciousness over the landscape of experience [Fox 1999]) are significant newer perspectives in reading Ecclesiastes. 'Meaning is genre dependent'—this sound interpretive guideline provides pointers and directives to how the book should be read. Further, readers may gain insights as to how individual sections that are of different literary genres and apparently fragmented are connected to the whole book through the literary clues. The whole is always larger than the sum of its parts. This presents yet another challenge in understanding Ecclesiastes, a book that is composed of a variety of genres. Our task is, hopefully, putting them together as an intentionally fabulous, cohesive whole.

B. Authorship and Dating

Few scholars today still support a Solomonic authorship, though the 'I'-voice in 1.2 and 1.12–2.16 is most naturally understood as Solomon, who was king in Jerusalem in the tenth century BCE. Arguments for a non-Solomonic anonymous figure are based on the following textual observations (see Longman III 1998: 4-9). *First,* the actual identity of the author is deliberately obscured (Heim 2019: 1-2). Unlike the case of Proverbs and Song of Songs, he is not named as Solomon but *Qohelet* instead (1.1, 2, 12; 7.27; 12.8, 9, 10). The root meaning of the Hebrew word *Qohelet* (it appears only in this book) is 'to assemble'. With the article 'the' in 12.8 (i.e. 'the Qohelet') and the dominant 'I'-voice spoken in the book, this Qohelet is likely to occupy a well-established social role, a professional title (i.e. the one who preaches in an assembly/the preacher). To the first audience, this intentional anonymity is perhaps to protect the preacher from the ruling power at that time (e.g. the critique of kingship in the book in 4.1-3; 5.8-9 [MT 7-8]; 8.2-9; 10.20). Yet, for the readers of today, its impact could be more profound. The preacher takes on the persona of a historical figure, Solomon, and speaks in an exceptional, personal style ('I, Qohelet'). He is calling for centuries of audiences to identify with his flesh-and-blood lived experience under the sun (1.12–2.26), and to share his meditative reflections because of his self-engaged quest for life and its realities (e.g. 3.16-4.16; 5.13-17 [MT 12-16]; 6.1-6; 7.15–10.7).

Second, Linguistic evidence indicates a non-Solomonic dating of Ecclesiastes. The presence of Persian loanwords, traces of Aramaic influence on the book, the abundance of economic terms employed, as well as the development of the language and style of the book place the earliest date of Ecclesiastes in the exilic or postexilic era. A postexilic date is the most common position held by scholars across the ideological spectrum. While C.L. Seow proposes a more specific timeframe within the fourth (or even fifth century; Seow 1997: 643-66), and John Goldingay suggests that the book fits the Persian more than the Hellenistic era (Goldingay 2021a: 27), overwhelming evidence does support a dating in the final decades of the third century BCE (Heim 2019: 4-5; see the discussion in Krüger 2004: 19-21). The latest date for the book is set by the fragments of the book among the Dead Sea Scrolls (4QQoh) found in Qumran, which suggest a date between 175 and 150 BCE. The implication then is that Ecclesiastes must have been written about 200 BCE.

Since there is no textual reference or external historical evidence for the dating of Ecclesiastes, the precise dating of the book remains largely undetermined. Putting the authorship and dating issue together into consideration, I propose here that the author of the book is primarily the Qohelet who takes on the Solomonic persona. As with the composition of any memoir, the editor provides a framing device for the narration (1.1-2a; 7.7; 12.8). Qohelet himself (or the editor) adds on wisdom sayings in strategic junctions all along his first-person meditative reflections to provide a theological framework for the discourse. *Carpe diem* sayings are inserted to provide the 'God-given/-demanded' notion for the enjoyment of life despite the harshness of life under the sun. Qohelet's speech begins with his motto in 1.1 and ends in 12.8. A final editor (the epilogist) is compelled to supplement the whole with some *correctives* to end the book, seeking to make it right for the audience (esp. after the agonizing cry in 12.8). Perceiving Qohelet as the author, as a real person behind the literary persona, the book powerfully presents to us an individual who is exceptionally personal and transparent, a constant consciousness that is deeply rooted in humanity's flesh-and-blood lived experience under the sun. He is inviting today's audience for our readerly responses to the book.

Alternatively, drawing on the power of imagination, Goldingay seeks to approach the issue of whether Qohelet is a real person or merely a literary creation. To him, 'Ecclesiastes is a collection of testimonies and observations that half-invites readers to think they come from Solomon' ('half-invites' in that the book does not name him; Goldingay 2021b: 25). In like manner, Ecclesiastes takes a historical figure (Solomon) at its debut and then composes a work of imagination. Since it is 'inspired imagination', the lived experiences and observations behind the figure Qohelet are to be perceived as authentic.

C. Ecclesiastes as Wisdom Literature

Narrowly defined, together with the books of Proverbs and Job, Ecclesiastes is among the wisdom literature in the Old Testament. Albeit scholarly efforts in the past decades sought to define 'wisdom', we still have not arrived at a common consensus. What we share, however, are observations of the characteristics of wisdom literature (esp. among the three commonly recognized wisdom books in the Old Testament). Current development in wisdom scholarship is moving toward a more anthropocentric focus (cf. Kessler 2013: 443-506; Goldingay 2009: 583-707). In keeping with the objectives of this 'Readings' series, my focus will be on the literary characteristics and prominent subject matters discussed among the three books, with specific focus on Ecclesiastes. On the literary dimension, Ecclesiastes shares with the other two books the following literary features: (1) the drive of narrating (e.g. 1.1-21; 1.12–2.26; 3.16–4.16; 5.13 [MT 12]–6.6; 7.15–10.7); (2) frequent use of rhetorical questions (e.g. 1.10; 2.12, 15, 25; 3.21-22); (3) traditional proverbial sayings (e.g. 4.5-6, 9-14; 5.1-7 [MT 4.17–5.6]); and (4) the use of metaphors (e.g. the metaphor *hebel*). Moreover, wisdom literature is both theocentric and anthropocentric. Its message places a distance, a mysterious realm between the creator God who is in heaven and humanity who dwell on earth. The catchword 'under the sun' appears everywhere in Ecclesiastes (e.g. 5.2b [5.1b]; 9.13).

Advocating that wisdom theology is creation theology, Leo G. Perdue has insightfully proposed a reading agenda for the study of wisdom books. To him, the dialectic of anthropocentric and theocentric represents the best approach to the theology of wisdom. Perdue further affirms that it should be perceived as a true dialectic, and not as a development from one (theocentric) to another (anthropocentric), or from an emphasis on one to a greater stress on the other (see Perdue 1994: 34-48). Moreover, he points out that certain wisdom books may have a more anthropocentric or theocentric emphasis. This perception has profound implications on our approach to the interpretation of and thus the message of Ecclesiastes. My view is, Ecclesiastes affirms both the anthropocentric and theocentric emphases, though it appears to be utterly human-centered through the driving force of the narrating 'I'-voice of Qohelet (e.g. 'I turned and saw', 4.1; 'I have seen', 6.1). It puts much focus on the 'order of things' as set out by *the creator God in heaven* (e.g. 1.4-11; 3.1-8) and the *disorderly chaos* of this 'order' as witnessed in *humanity's collective lived experience under the sun* (see e.g. 7.15; 8.14). The conflicts between the two, God's 'order of ruling' and humanity's 'lived experience', are in true dialectic within the book. Our task is not to resolve the tensions nor to make the rough places smooth. Perhaps, as life's repertoire, seeking the 'hows' of embracing coexisting tensions as normative for humans to live under the sun should be the goal. As Michael V. Fox has rightly pointed out, 'I too take Qohelet's contradictions as the starting point for interpretation. My thesis is a simple one: The contradictions in the book of Qohelet are real and intended. We should interpret them, not eliminate them' (Fox 1999: 3).

D. Message

With a text-anchored and reader-oriented approach to interpretation, we can hardly speak of 'the' message of Ecclesiastes. Meaning-making comes at the intersection between text and reader. Paying due attention to the text, readers engage themselves in the meaning-making process out of their own contextual situatedness. Craig G. Bartholomew has precisely pointed out the state of the inquiry. Despite all the historical work done on the book, scholars remain undecided as to whether the book is basically a pessimistic or optimistic book (1998: 3).

On another front, Heim coins the term 'underdetermination' and proposes that the book's use of 'underdetermined language' is intentional. Just like the expressions used by modern stand-up comedians, this kind of 'indirection', vague language, leaves more room for readers to construct their own meaning of the book. Just like the indirection expressions made by modern stand-up comedians, there is a certain openness for the audience to understand its meaning. Therefore, one cannot legitimately speak of 'the' meaning/message of the book (Heim 2019: 5).

With the focus on the Qohelet behind the 'I'-voice, a majority of scholars still hold to the position that Qohelet is a disillusioned sceptic who challenges orthodox beliefs. At the opposite end of the spectrum, others see the book's protagonist as an orthodox teacher with a positive view of life (see Longman 1998: 31 n. 119). Recent commentators have taken a more anthropocentric focus on the book's message. Heim is of the view that the book's message has the capacity to strengthen the simplistic and naive kind of faith amid adversity (Heim, 4). On the surface, the book is a theological debate on the purpose of life. Yet on a deeper level, the book's message is deeply rooted in the first audience's painful experiences under repressive regimes (Heim, 9). 'It is a missive of hope, a rallying cry to cultural resistance, an appeal to remain faithful to God' (Heim, 9). Goldingay sees that the book challenges readers to reconsider what they think life is about and how it is possible to understand God's involvement in the world. More significantly, Ecclesiastes disturbs the optimistic and yet uplifts the gloomy (Goldingay 2021a: 53-54). The book also moves readers to rethink 'how to live' seriously. As Peter Enns has boldly noted, Ecclesiastes has a significant role in the Bible in that 'it affirms the normalcy and benefit of being in a state of struggle, despair and disorientation in one's relationship with God' (Enns 2011: 207). Undoubtedly, reading Ecclesiastes in the third decade of the twenty-first century, we are gifted with open possibilities and newer windows of perception through the exemplary interpretive efforts in the recent past.

I have taken a two-focus approach to uncovering the message of the book: anthropocentric and theocentric. With a two-edged sword as my primary interpretive tool, the *dialectic* between 'the order of God's ruling' and 'the chaotic disorder of humanity's lived experience', I seek to dissect the book through the integration of five reading strategies. In most cases, the question you ask will determine the answer you get. I seek to provide pointers and directives to my readers as we journey through the twelve chapters of meaning-making, asking appropriate questions of the text. If the central message of Ecclesiastes is about 'how to live', my proposal is: 'Embracing coexisting dialectic tensions that are of polar nature is the way to live'. Taking this as one of the proposed meanings of the book, readers are challenged to always seek to strike the balance between the two poles: 'embracing absurdity' and 'joy-seeking', as each of us journeys through life, taking on whatever comes along the way.

Approaching Ecclesiastes: Reading Strategies

Unpacking the complexity of Ecclesiastes entails the working out of an integrated approach toward interpretation. This effort will open new windows of perception and provide legitimate 'points of entry' for understanding. Five intentionally hammered out reading strategies will be employed in this commentary—reading narratively, reading polyphonically, reading dialectically, reading 'cross the grains' and reading Ecclesiastes as a memoir. These are not five competing strategies of reading, but interconnected perspectives toward interpreting the book as a cohesive whole. I seek to demonstrate that through the interweaving of these five perspectival readings, it will further enrich and expand the meaning-significance of Ecclesiastes.

A. Reading Narratively

The self-narrating dynamic of Ecclesiastes is a distinctive feature of the book. In coining the term 'Narratival Hermeneutics [hermeneutics= the science of interpretation]', Canadian contributors to the 2019 collection *Reading In-between: How Minoritized Cultural Minorities Interpret the Bible in Canada* (Medina, Kim-Cragg, Hari-Singh 2019) came up with demonstrated examples of 'narrative hermeneutics' through their collaborative efforts (see e.g. Leung Lai 2019b: 36-51; Yorke 2019: 112-21). As a working agenda, 'narrative hermeneutics' is an interpretive path that takes seriously the flesh-and-blood lived experience of the first readers as well as the community of contemporary readers as the contexts of interpretation. As a commonly accepted maxim, 'all content is subject to context, and there is no text without context' (Fetzer and Oishi 2011: 171). The commonality of this 'cross-culture and time' reading is found in humanity's lived experience 'under the sun'. Ecclesiastes is utterly anthropocentric. The personal experience, reflections, explorations, inner debates and summary appraisals of Qohelet are not 'imagined' realities/narratives. They are rooted in the flesh-and-blood *collective* human experience under the sun. Appropriating such a reading strategy to Ecclesiastes has proven to be very fruitful. The case in point is that the vibrant dynamics and power of the *art* and *science* of 'Narratival Hermeneutics' could be brought to the foreground through such endeavor.

The 'I'-discourse portion of the book provides us with a step-by-step guidebook in formulating the significant episodes of Qohelet's 'text-of-life'. These steps are not merely life's important milestones but layers of *cumulative*, empirical wisdom. The cycle of 'turning → seeing → reflecting → perceiving → concluding' (e.g. 1.14-18; 2.1-11, 12-26; 3.16-22; 4.1-3, 4-6, 7-10, 11-12, 15-16; 5.13-20 [MT 12-19]; 6.1-12; 7.15-18, 25-29; 8.10-12, 14-17; 9.1-10, 11-12, 13-18; 10.5-15; cf. Leung Lai 2014: 214-16) characterizes Qohelet's persistent self-engagement in life. From the intentional and self-initiated *'turning'* (e.g. 4.1, 7) to a deep level of commitment (e.g. 8.16, 'When I gave my heart to know wisdom, and to see the task that is done on the earth—people getting no sleep day or night') signifies a dynamic process of self-engagement. The components in this cycle of life-exploration are not derived from a mechanical step-by-step manual. They exemplify the lively dynamics of a seeker, an explorer of life (e.g. 'Again I looked and saw …', 4.1; 'Behold, this is what I have observed to be good …', 5.18 [MT 17]).

With the shared common denominator of the 'collective lived experience under the sun', readers can echo each of the anguished cries of Qohelet and the deep-rooted, burdensome (though at times, uplifting) concluding statements he utters. The ideological reflections are not constructed sophistically or after a rigid frame of reference. Rather, they are anchored in the flesh-and-blood collective lived experience of all humanity. The *power* and *dynamics* of these observations, narrations, reflections and conclusions help to underscore the *what*s in life's realities and the *how*s in embracing the coexisting dialectic tensions. Reading Ecclesiastes narratively is, at the same time, laying out a robust drama of the dogma rooted in humanity's collective lived experience under the sun. This can be referred to as the *Grand Narrative* that each of us shares and continuously contributes to slices (or components) of its reality.

Qohelet's captivating 'I'-voice, the mode of narration (i.e. the cycle of exploration), the unreserved sharing of his inner thoughts (in a sense, inner debates, e.g. 1.16; 2.1; 3.18) and his tormented cries lie raw in front of all contemporary audiences and thus close the gap between a highly sophisticated character Qohelet and the reader of today.

B. Reading Polyphonically

The interface of voice and ideology is firmly established in the field of biblical studies (see Greenwood 2012: 476-91; Landy 2000: 19-36; 2004:

113-51; Leung Lai 2013: 265-78). Ecclesiastes is predominantly an 'I'-text (i.e. one in which the main character speaks in the first-person 'I'-voice), but it is also multivoiced. Identification of the different voices represented in Ecclesiastes has been an area of interest in the recent past. A total of five voices have been identified in this polyphony. *First* is the voice of the sages, regarded as the 'true voice of wisdom', which primarily narrates in the second-person (e.g. 1.3-11; 3.1-8; 4.5-6, 9-14). It represents the wisdom tradition in ancient Israel (or the embedded ideology of Ecclesiastes, i.e. Qohelet's pretext). The *second* voice is the voice of Qohelet speaking in the enchanting first-person 'I'-voice (e.g. 1.12-15, 17-18; 2.3-14; 4.1-4). It signifies the reshaped ideology of Qohelet, which is cast in sharp contrast to the ideology ingrained in the text (i.e. the wisdom tradition). The *third* voice serves as the 'frame narrator' and is found in the third-person sections of chs. 1, 7 and 12 (1.1-2a; 7.27a; 12.8a). The *fourth* voice is the inner voice of Qohelet, which emerges from imaginary dialogues within monologues (e.g. 'I said in my heart saying, I, behold'; 1.16; 2.1-2; 2.15; 3.17). The *fifth* is the voice of the epilogist in 12.9-14, who seeks to provide a quick fix to the surfaced tensions from 1.1 to 12.8 through Qohelet's search for meaning.

Along this interpretive path, there is another voice, the interpretive voice of the reader representing the readerly ideology we bring to the text, interacting with the embedded textual ideologies of traditional wisdom and the reshaped ideology of Qohelet. Therefore, there are potentially six voices/sets of ideology engaging in vibrant interaction with one another, both dialogically and dialectically (i.e. creating conflicting opinions through lively dialogues).

Considering polyphony as the characteristic feature of Ecclesiastes, the analysis and textual dynamics of narration, reflection, inner debate, elucidation and resolution (especially the role of the epilogist in 12.9-14) take on new dimensions of meaning. Moreover, the intertwining of speaking voices in Ecclesiastes provides a framing for reading and *hearing* the text (i.e. 'the hermeneutics of hearing', which can be appropriately applied to the interpretation of a polyphonic text; see Snodgrass 2002: 1-32).

The multivoices engaging in lively dialogues within the twelve chapters underscore the nature of the textual dynamics of Ecclesiastes. Russian literary theorist Mikhael Bakhtin's notion of polyphony and dialogism provides significant impact on the reading of this polyphonic book (see Bakhtin 1984; 1986a; 1986b; Newsom 1996: 290-306; 2002: 87-108; Leung Lai 2011: 13-42, esp. 19-22). Furthermore, the appropriation of the so-called Bakhtinian 'dialogic truth' has profound implications for grasping the meaning of the text through the polyphonic-dialogic mode of expression in the book. To elaborate further, the Bakhtinian perception of 'dialogic truth' introduces a whole new dimension of the function of Qohelet's monologic/dialogic discourse, including the 'saying in his own heart' (e.g. 1.15; 2.1, 15). As pioneers of speaking voice analysis, Meir Sternberg, and L. Alonso Schökel have succeeded in exemplifying 'monologue/dialogue' in the Hebrew Bible (see Sternberg 1986: 295-318; Alonso Schökel 1998: 178). Contained in the pericope are pockets of monologue within dialogues and imaginary dialogues within monologues. In fact, one can collapse the distinction between monologue and dialogue as they serve the same function of self-representation. Alonso Schökel further qualifies monologue as 'the breaking into a context of dialogue with a reflection directed to oneself' (Alonso Schökel 1998: 81).

Ecclesiastes is a polyphony, and it is also an "I"-text in which Qohelet speaks in the first-person 'I'-voice all the time. This dialogic-interacting dynamic fits in beautifully with Qohelet's monologic-dialogic mode of expression. Qohelet is entering freely into vibrant dialogue with the other speaking voices—that of the frame narrator (1.1-2; 7.27a; 12.8), the collective voice of the sages (the traditional wisdom), his own 'inner voice' and the voice of the epilogist in 12.9-14. It is through this 'dialogue', the textual dynamic of the merged, that is, Qohelet's inner voice (e.g. 1.16; 2.1-2, 15) and unmerged speaking voices that the Bakhtinian 'dialogic truth' is distinctively brought to the foreground and the moral of the text is to be attained.

C. Reading Dialectically

Fox notes insightfully that the purpose of interpreting Ecclesiastes is not to avoid the existing tensions nor to seek to eliminate the contradictions (Fox 1999: 3). In fact, Ecclesiastes is a book engrained with dialectic tensions that are of a polar nature (e.g. 'the heart of the wise' and 'the heart of the fool' [7.1-5]; 'the righteous perishing' and 'the wicked living long' [7.15]; 'the righteous get what the wicked deserve, the wicked get what the righteous deserve' [8.14]). Three observations can be obtained in unloading this statement.

First, Qohelet holds on to the ideology that all attempts to search for the 'order of things' in this chaotic world will be met with sheer disappointment (7.15-28; 8.12, 14; 12.8). As a resistant explorer of realities laid out in classical wisdom, Qohelet's loud remark in 10.5 touches the core and true dynamics of his search for the 'order of things': 'There is an evil I have seen under the sun, like an error that comes from a ruler'. The ideology ingrained in the text—'Fear God and keep his commandments'—is required of all humanity (12.13). Qohelet seeks to embrace both in *all flesh* but finds it burdensome and oppressive (see esp. 10.1; 8.16). The epilogist seeks to defend the latter by underscoring, twice in the 'afterword', the expressions 'And more than that ...' (12.9) and 'more than these ...' (12.12). Two sets of ideologies are presented side by side. My attempt is neither seeking to harmonize (or synthesize) the two conflicting ideologies nor picking one against the other as an interpretive choice. As we journey through the interpretation of the book, I aim at guiding my readers with pointers and directives—putting both conflicting ideologies side by side as a *coexisting* reality.

Second, dialectic inner tensions exist in Qohelet's formulation and development of his ideology rooted in the commonality of humanity's collective lived experience under the sun. On the one hand, Qohelet affirms the sovereignty and justice of God over the absurdity and nonsensicality of human life (see 2.26; 3.10-11, 14-15; 7.18, 29; 8.11-13; 9.1 in their immediate contexts). On the other hand, he is overwhelmed by the collapse of the 'order of thing' in the realities of human existence. He seeks to embrace these coexisting dialectic tensions in *all flesh*.

Third, the presence of the seven uplifting, kerygmatic *carpe diem* sayings (2.24-25; 3.12-13; 3.22; 5.18-20 [MT 17-19]; 8.15; 9.7-10; 11.9-10) amidst Qohelet's pessimistic 'I'-discourse, which run through the twelve chapters until 12.8, creates another dialectic tension. The magnitude of the absurdity in life (3.16-17; 7.15; 8.12-14) drives Qohelet to a weighty summary appraisal: seeking to make some sense out of the nonsensicality in life is like 'a chasing after the wind', doomed to fail! These seven sayings encourage readers to 'seize the day' and live life fully before God with all its enjoyments. They are good gifts from God—our lot/portion. The seven sayings appear sparingly within the book. Somehow, they break the main line of thought and are at odds with the dialogic dynamics of the book. Their appearance thus causes some concerns for the structure and coherence of the whole book. Even in the context of the dialectic momentum within the text, the sayings are uplifting, encouraging, appealing and rooted in the flesh-and-blood lived experience of the community of Israel. Their appearance affirms the other side of the reality: amidst the nonsensicality of life, there is still the call to 'live life along with all its enjoyments, for they are God's good gifts'. Qohelet embraces both realities (absurdity and enjoyment of life) in all *flesh*. In 2.17-18, Qohelet declares that he hates life ('Therefore, I hated life. . . . Yes, I hated all my labor that I labor under the sun'); this declaration adds on another layer of tension in the light of the overarching dialectic feature of Ecclesiastes.

D. Reading 'Cross the Grains'

Using the imagery of woodwork, all texts, just like wood, are said to have grains, or directionality. I have picked up Carol A. Newsom's 'plywood' analogy here but with a more focused appropriation (see Newsom 2009: 553-57). Along the ideological-critical path of any given text, there are two conventional reading strategies, namely, reading 'with the grain' and 'reading against the grain'.

For ideological-critical endeavours, reading 'against the grain' seems to be the norm. Engaging Ecclesiastes calls for a reading that is crossing the grains. 'Cross-graining' is applied to the production of plywood by gluing together layers (veneers) of adjacent piles having the wood grain at a right angles to each other to form a high quality, good-strength wood panel. Specifically, plywood is bonded with the grain of one layer running perpendicular to the grain direction of another. Thus, several thin layers of wood bonded together would be stronger than one single thick layer of wood. It produces the strongest kind of wood, which is hard to bend. I have found the 'cross-graining' imagery quite fitting to a reading strategy for Ecclesiastes. 'Cross-graining' incorporates both conventional 'against the grain' and 'with the grain' readings and has the potential of moving toward a multilayered, more enriching meaning-significance of the book.

There are subsequently four potential ideologies represented in 'cross-graining' by engaged readers: (1) the ideology of traditional wisdom to which Qohelet is interacting 'against the grain' (e.g. 7.15; 8.14); (2) the multilayered ideology upheld by Qohelet and rooted in his community's collective lived experience (e.g. 4.1-3, 4-6, 7-12); (3) the reshaped ideology proposed by the frame narrator and especially by the epilogist in 12.9-14, which counteracts the ideology presented by Qohelet; and (4) the invited ideology as a result of 'cross-graining'—navigating through the options of one's interpretive choice and negotiating by placing the existing interpretive tensions side by side as an enriched whole (cf. Leung Lai 2013: 265-78).

The imagery of the production of plywood fits beautifully in reading Ecclesiastes. I aim at guiding my readers in uncovering the existence of the many cross-graining fibres that constitute the book—that is, the multi-faceted components that make up its collective message.

E. Reading as a 'Memoir'

Notwithstanding the identity behind the 'I'-voice in Ecclesiastes, which is still an unsettling issue to some, Qohelet's long discourse is laden with strong emotions. Sometimes they are subtly expressed (e.g. 7.23-24; 10.5-7); other times they are explosive (e.g. 2.17-19; 12.8). The deep reflective nature of Qohelet's narration, his investigative spirit, his shared rich experiences in life, and, more distinctively, his bold and affirmative statement that life is utterly absurd—all point to the driving force behind Qohelet's self-narrative. They are not spur-of-the-moment responses, nor the outpouring of anguished cries triggered by specific incidences in life. It is neither a merely thinking-out-loud mode of expression, nor a well-organized recollection of his life experiences. Rather, Qohelet narrates as a memoirist, recollecting significant milestones of his lived experience under the sun. He recounts his *personal* life accomplishments (1.12–2.26), and shares with deep reflection the results of his exploration in life (3.16–4.16; 5.13 [MT 5.12]–7.12; 7.15–10.7).

Reading Ecclesiastes as Qohelet's memoir opens new dimensions of meaning for the first readers as well as for readers of today. It adds on the didactic function of the book. This is accomplished with the final editor providing a framing for the narration (the third-person frame narrator). On several occasions, Qohelet interacts with his pretext—traditional wisdom—and engages in lively dialogue with the other voices—that of the epilogist and through doubling himself up in two halves, debating with his inner thoughts (i.e. his inner voice). This memoir is rich and deeply rooted in his personal as well as his community's *flesh-and-blood* lived experience (i.e. autoethnography: linking the personal account with the community of the first readers). The whole generates a highly captivating and inviting force to all contemporary readers to identify self-engagingly with this *Grand Narrative*.

In what ways would a memoir-reading prove to be more enriching? Recent studies on writing personal narratives in social sciences and the humanities have contributed greatly to the understanding of memoir as a biblical genre. Some of the recent advances could be appropriated to analyzing the structure of Nehemiah (e.g. Leung Lai 2015) and the book of Deuteronomy (as Moses's memoir; see A.J. Culp 2019). *First,* as a provocative genre, memoir focuses on a particular emotional relationship in the author's past, an intimate narrative concerned more with *who* is remembering and *why* than with *what* is remembered (Larson 2007: summary). Writing a memoir challenges the author to disclose one's deepest *self* through the 'I'-narration. It thus provides a channel, a platform for the memoirist to release one's heightened emotive responses, be it grief, joy, helplessness, laments whose purpose no other literary vehicle could fulfil (perhaps, to a certain extent, through poetry). As it is often said, a memoir is not *of* a memoirist, nor *to* the author, but rather *for* the author—the one writing the memoir—to serve one's agenda. From another perspective, Mary Maguire comments that we define ourselves by what we remember of our 'selves'; thus the subject and object are the same (Maguire 2006: article16). A memoirist touches on the nuances of memory, of finding and telling the truth, and of disclosing one's deepest *self*. Reading Ecclesiastes as Qohelet's memoir helps readers to empathize with his deep-rooted tormented cries through his summary appraisals (e.g. 1.2; 12.8); to appreciate the silent release of his feelings of puzzlement (e.g. 2.15; 8.16, 17); and to capture his emotions in the face of dialectic tensions (e.g. 7.15; 8.14).

Second, memoir is nonfiction written in the first person about a 'slice of life'. In contrast to autobiography, which is expected to tell everything, a memoir tells something that is related to the chosen topic. Reading Ecclesiastes from the perspective of a memoirist, the subject matter is about *human experience under the sun*. Memoir is truth, and every piece of this truth is filtered through one's experience. The goal for writing a memoir should be to write as authentically and as honestly as possible, so that the truth resonates with the readers on the universal level (i.e. the Grand Narrative). As Louisa Deasey has noted, the reason why many people read memoirs is to know how the author dealt with a particular problem, situation or life experience on a detailed and personal level, and come to some sense of conclusion or resolution about it at the end (Deasey 2018). Reading Ecclesiastes as a memoir, Qohelet is not to be perceived as a literary persona, nor the twelve chapters as hypothetical case studies ending with more philosophical reflections or ready-made resolutions (e.g. 12.9-14). It is anchored in the flesh-and-blood collective human experience under the sun, of which all humanity can identify with slices of its own reality.

Third, a successful memoir *shows,* not only *tells,* a personal story. Journalists *tell* the facts in the exposition of a story, but memoirists do a lot more work; they engage in psychological deep-diving and *showing* (Deasey 2018). I find this observation quite inspiring. As with the narrator of any given biblical narrative, the *hows* of the story narrated are more important than the *whats*. Good *showing* is found alongside Qohelet's *telling* in his memoir through interior monologue (1.16; 2.1-2; 2.15); motion verbs instead of mere narration (e.g. 2.4-9); silent verbs of action ('I saw', 'I turned and saw'—e.g. 2.12; 3.22; 4.4; 5.13 [MT 12]; 7.15; 10.5); and perhaps, an invitation to all readers to look into his mind and heart (e.g. 8.16; 9.1). An engaged reader would find in this Qohelet's memoir that the *showing* part is far more intentional than the *telling*. Readers get the message that it is Qohelet the memoirist's intent for us to be in touch with his feelings, his deep reflective thoughts and the paradoxical situation he is facing. He intends to provoke, to stir up, to disturb and to disrupt readers about life and how best to cope with it.

Reading Qohelet's memoir liberates generations of readers from the constraint of interpretive issues (e.g. authorship, identifying the primary literary genre, whether the book is basically pessimistic or optimistic, etc.). Readers are drawn to Qohelet's inner life, his dilemmas, his troubling thoughts, and diving deep into his emotive responses out of his lived experience under the sun—of which, perhaps, we all share a slice of its realities. Reading Ecclesiastes is, at the same time, reading our 'selves'.

Text and Analysis of Speaking Voices

Remarks

1. Unless otherwise specified in the footnotes, or for gender-inclusive purposes, the translation is from the New International Version (NIV) Holy Bible, copyright © 1973, 1978, 1984, 2011 by Biblica, Inc.
2. To enhance the impact on readers in reading this polyphonic book, the analysis of different speaking voices has been highlighted in accordance with the following legend:

   UPPERCASE BOLD = The third-person frame narrator
   Bold Italics = Qohelet/the Preacher's inner voice
   Italics = The second-person collective voice of traditional wisdom (= Qohelet's 'Pretext')
   Bold = Voice of the epilogist
   Non-highlighted = Qohelet's first-person 'I' voice

3. For study groups, I highly recommend reading the book aloud dialogically through the voice analysis as presented here, assign members of the group to represent each of the five speaking voices in the book and the others as audience.

Chapters 1–12

1

THE WORDS OF THE PREACHER (QOHELET[1]). SON OF DAVID, KING IN JERUSALEM:

---

1. 'Qohelet' is the transliteration of the Hebrew word that bears the root meaning of 'one who convenes an assembly'. Qohelet/the preacher represents the primary 'I'-speaking voice within the book. The Hebrew word *Qohelet* is used in this commentary to distinguish it from the name of the book of Ecclesiastes.

² 'Vanity of vanities!'²
   SAYS QOHELET.
   'Vanity of vanities!'
   'All is vanity!'
³ What do people gain from all their labors
   at which they toil under the sun?

⁴ *Generations come and generations go,*
   but the earth remains forever.
⁵ *The sun rises and the sun sets,*
   and hurries back to where it rises.
⁶ *The wind blows to the south*
   and turns to the north;
  round and round it goes,
   ever returning on its course.
⁷ *All streams flow into the sea,*
   yet the sea is never full.
  To the place the streams come from,
   there they return again.
⁸ *All things are wearisome,*
   more than one can say.
  The eye never has enough of seeing,
   nor the ear its fill of hearing.
⁹ *What has been will be again,*
   what has been done will be done again;
   there is nothing new under the sun.
¹⁰ *Is there anything of which one can say,*
   'Look! This is something new'?
  It was here already, long ago;
   it was here before our time.
¹¹ *No one remembers the former generations,*
   and even those yet to come
  will not be remembered
   by those who follow them.

¹² I, the Teacher, was king over Israel in Jerusalem. ¹³ I applied my heart[3] to study and to explore by wisdom all that is done under the heavens. What

---

   2. My preferred translation of the Hebrew word (*hbl*) is 'vanity' instead of 'meaningless'.
   3. The Hebrew word used is 'heart'.

a heavy burden God has laid on humanity! ¹⁴ I have seen all the things that are done under the sun; and behold⁴, all is vanity, a chasing after the wind.

¹⁵ What is crooked cannot be straightened;
  what is lacking cannot be counted.

¹⁶ *I said in my heart⁵, 'Behold, I have increased in wisdom more than anyone who has ruled over Jerusalem before me; I have experienced much of wisdom and knowledge'.* ¹⁷ Then I applied myself to the understanding of wisdom, and also of madness and folly, but I learned that this, too, is a chasing after the wind.

¹⁸ For with much wisdom comes much sorrow;
  the more knowledge, the more grief.

2

I said to my heart, 'Come now, I will test you with pleasure to find out what is good'. But behold, this too is vanity. ² 'Laughter', I said, 'is madness. And what does pleasure accomplish?' ³ I tried cheering myself with wine and embracing folly—my mind still guiding me with wisdom. I wanted to see what was good for people to do under the heavens during the few days of their lives.

⁴ I undertook great projects: I built houses for myself and planted vineyards. ⁵ I made gardens and parks and planted all kinds of fruit trees in them. ⁶ I made reservoirs to water groves of flourishing trees. ⁷ I bought male and female slaves and had other slaves who were born in my house. I also owned more herds and flocks than anyone in Jerusalem before me. ⁸ I amassed silver and gold for myself, and the treasure of kings and provinces. I acquired male and female singers, and a harem as well—the delights of a man's heart. ⁹ I became greater by far than anyone in Jerusalem before me. In all this my wisdom stayed with me.

¹⁰ I denied myself nothing my eyes desired;
  I refused my heart no pleasure.
 My heart took delight in all my labor,
  and this was the reward for all my toil.

---

4. 'And behold' represents the captivating force in the Hebrew text, left untranslated in NIV.
5. Literally, 'I spoke with my heart'.

¹¹ Yet when I surveyed all that my hands had done
>   and what I had toiled to achieve,
> and behold, all was vanity, a chasing after the wind;
>   nothing was gained under the sun.
¹² Then I turned my thoughts to consider wisdom,
>   and also madness and folly.
> What more can the king's successor do
>   than what has already been done?
¹³ I saw that wisdom is better than folly,
>   just as light is better than darkness.
¹⁴ The wise have eyes in their heads,
>   while the fool walks in the darkness;
> but I came to realize
>   that the same fate overtakes them both.

¹⁵ Then I said to myself,
> *'The fate of the fool will overtake me also.*
>   *What then do I gain by being wise?'*
> *I said to myself,*
>   *'This too is meaningless'.*
¹⁶ For the wise, like the fool, will not be long remembered;
>   *the days have already come when both have been forgotten.*
> *And how does the wise die like the fool!*⁶

¹⁷ So I hated life, because the work that is done under the sun was grievous to me. All is vanity, a chasing after the wind. ¹⁸ I hated all the things I had toiled for under the sun, because I must leave them to the one who comes after me. ¹⁹ And who knows whether that person will be wise or foolish? Yet they will have control over all the fruit of my toil into which I have poured my effort and skill under the sun. This too is vanity. ²⁰ So my heart began to despair over all my toilsome labor under the sun. ²¹ For a person may labor with wisdom, knowledge, and skill, and then they must leave all they own to another who has not toiled for it. This too is vanity and a great misfortune. ²² What do people get for all the toil and anxious striving with which they labor under the sun? ²³ All their days their work is grief and pain; even at night their minds do not rest. This too is vanity.

²⁴ A person can do nothing better than to eat and drink and find satisfaction in their own toil. This too, I see, is from the hand of God, ²⁵ for without

---

6. Literal translation of the Hebrew text.

him, who can eat or find enjoyment? ²⁶ To the person who pleases him, God gives wisdom, knowledge, and happiness, but to the sinner he gives the task of gathering and storing up wealth to hand it over to the one who pleases God. This too is vanity, a chasing after the wind.

3

There is a time for everything,
* and a season for every activity under the heavens:*
² *a time to be born and a time to die,*
* a time to plant and a time to uproot,*
³ *a time to kill and a time to heal,*
* a time to tear down and a time to build,*
⁴ *a time to weep and a time to laugh,*
* a time to mourn and a time to dance,*
⁵ *a time to scatter stones and a time to gather them,*
* a time to embrace and a time to refrain from embracing,*
⁶ *a time to search and a time to give up,*
* a time to keep and a time to throw away,*
⁷ *a time to tear and a time to mend,*
* a time to be silent and a time to speak,*
⁸ *a time to love and a time to hate,*
* a time for war and a time for peace.*

⁹ What do workers gain from their toil? ¹⁰ I have seen the burden God has laid on humanity with which to be preoccupied[7]. ¹¹ He has made everything beautiful in its time. He has also set eternity in the human heart; yet no one can fathom what God has done from beginning to end. ¹² I know that there is nothing better for people than to be happy and to do good while they live. ¹³ That each of them may eat and drink and find satisfaction in all their toil—this is the gift of God. ¹⁴ I know that everything God does will endure forever; nothing can be added to it, and nothing taken from it. God does it so that people will fear him.

¹⁵ Whatever is has already been,
  and what will be has been before;
  and God will call the past to account.

¹⁶ And I saw something else under the sun:

---

7. The latter part of v. 10 remains untranslated in NIV.

In the place of judgment—wickedness was there,
  in the place of justice—wickedness was there.

[17] I said to myself,

'God will bring into judgment
  both the righteous and the wicked,
for there will be a time for every activity,
  a time to judge every deed'.

[18] I also said to myself, 'As for humans, God tests them so that they may see that they are like the animals. [19] Surely the fate of human beings is like that of the animals; the same fate awaits them both: As one dies, so dies the other. All have the same breath; humans have no advantage over animals. Everything is meaningless. [20] All go to the same place; all come from dust, and to dust all return. [21] Who knows if the human spirit rises upward and if the spirit of the animal goes down into the earth?'

[22] So I saw that there is nothing better for humans than to enjoy their works, because that is their lot. For who can bring them to see what will happen after them?[8]

4

[1] Again I returned[9] and saw all the oppression that was taking place under the sun:
  I saw the tears of the oppressed—
    and they have no comforter;
  power was on the side of their oppressors—
    and they have no comforter.
[2] And I declared that the dead,
    who had already died,
  are happier than the living,
    who are still alive.
[3] But better than both
    is the one who has never been born,
  who has not seen the evil
    that is done under the sun.

---

    8. For gender-inclusive purpose, singular 'the man' changed to plural: 'humans', therefore, their/them, and 'works' in plural.
    9. Literally, 'I returned', in the sense of 'Again I turned and saw', beginning another cycle of exploration in life, also v. 7.

⁴ And I saw that all toil and all achievement spring from one person's envy of another. This too is vanity, a chasing after the wind.

⁵ *Fools fold their hands*
   and ruin themselves.
⁶ *Better one handful with tranquillity*
   than two handfuls with toil
   and chasing after the wind.

⁷ Again I returned and saw something meaningless under the sun:
⁸ There was a man all alone;
   he had neither son nor brother.
There was no end to his toil,
   yet his eyes were not content with his wealth.
'For whom am I toiling', he asked,
   'and why am I depriving myself of enjoyment?'¹⁰
This too is vanity—
   and an evil task!

⁹ *Two are better than one,*
   because they have a good return for their labor:
¹⁰ *If either of them falls down,*
   one can help the other up.
   But pity anyone who falls
   and has no one to help them up.
¹¹ *Also, if two lie down together, they will keep warm.*
   But how can one keep warm alone? ¹² *Two can defend themselves.*
   A cord of three strands is not quickly broken.

¹³ Better a poor but wise youth than an old but foolish king who no longer knows how to heed a warning. ¹⁴ The youth may have come from prison to the kingship, or he may have been born in poverty within his kingdom. ¹⁵ I saw that all who lived and walked under the sun followed the youth, the king's successor. ¹⁶ There was no end to all the people who were before them. But those who came later were not pleased with the successor. Surely¹¹ this too is vanity, a chasing after the wind.¹²

---

   10. Literally, 'depriving my soul from good'.
   11. Untranslated in NIV.
   12. The ambiguity of vv. 14-16 makes all translations and hence interpretations uncertain. NIV's translation here makes good sense to readers (see Murphy 1992: 40-43).

5

¹³ *Guard your steps when you go to the house of God. Go near to listen rather than to offer the sacrifice of fools, who do not know that they do wrong.*
² *Do not be quick with your mouth,*
 do not be hasty in your heart
 to utter anything before God.
 God is in heaven
 and you are on earth,
 so let your words be few.
³ *A dream comes when there are many cares,*
 and many words mark the speech of a fool.
⁴ *When you make a vow to God, do not delay to fulfill it. God has no pleasure in fools; fulfill your vow.* ⁵ *It is better not to make a vow than to make one and not fulfill it.* ⁶ *Do not let your mouth lead you into sin. And do not protest to the temple messenger, 'My vow was a mistake'. Why should God be angry at what you say and destroy the work of your hands?* ⁷ *Much dreaming and many words are vanities. Therefore, fear God.*

⁸ *If you see the poor oppressed in a district, and justice and rights denied, do not be surprised at such things; for one official is eyed by a higher one, and over them both are others higher still.* ⁹ *The increase from the land is taken by all; the king himself profits from the fields.*

¹⁰ *Whoever loves money never has enough;*
 whoever loves wealth is never satisfied with their income.
 This too is vanity.
¹¹ *As goods increase,*
 so do those who consume them.
 And what benefit are they to the owners
 except to feast their eyes on them?
¹² *The sleep of a laborer is sweet,*
 whether they eat little or much,
 but as for the rich, their abundance
 permits them no sleep.

¹³ I have seen a grievous evil under the sun: Wealth hoarded to the harm
 of its owners,
¹⁴ or wealth lost through some misfortune,

---

13. 5.1-20 (MT 4.17–5.19).

> so that when they[14] have children
>> there is nothing left for them to inherit.
> [15] Everyone comes naked from their mother's womb,
>> and as everyone comes, so they depart.
> They take nothing from their toil
>> that they can carry in their hands.

[16] This too is a grievous evil:

> As everyone comes, so they depart,
>> and what do they gain,
>> since they toil for the wind?
> [17] All their days they eat in darkness,
>> with great frustration, affliction and anger.

[18] Behold![15] This is what I have observed to be good: that it is appropriate for a person to eat, to drink and to find satisfaction in their toilsome labor under the sun during the few days of life God has given them—for this is their lot. [19] Moreover, when God gives someone wealth and possessions, and the ability to enjoy them, to accept their lot and be happy in their toil—this is a gift of God. [20] They seldom reflect on the days of their life, because God keeps them occupied with gladness of heart.

6

[1] I have seen another evil under the sun, and it weighs heavily on humanity: [2] God gives some people wealth, possessions, and honor, so that they lack nothing their hearts desire, but God does not grant them the ability to enjoy them, and strangers enjoy them instead. This is vanity, a grievous evil.

[3] A person may have a hundred children and live many years; yet no matter how long he lives, if he cannot enjoy his prosperity and does not receive proper burial, I say that a stillborn child is better off than he. [4] It comes without meaning, it departs in darkness, and in darkness its name is shrouded. [5] Though it never saw the sun or knew anything, it has more rest than does that man— [6] even if he lives a thousand years twice over but fails to enjoy his prosperity. Do not all go to the same place?

> [7] Everyone's toil is for their mouth,
>> yet their appetite is never satisfied.

---

14. The personal pronouns from vv. 13-17 [MT 12-16] are all in the third-person singular. For gender-inclusive purposes, the translations here are in the third-person plural.

15. Untranslated in NIV.

⁸ What advantage have the wise over fools?
  What do the poor gain
    by knowing how to conduct themselves before others?
⁹ Better what the eye sees
    than the roving of the appetite.
  This too is vanity,
    a chasing after the wind.
¹⁰ Whatever exists has already been named,
    and what humanity is has been known;
  no one can contend
    with someone who is stronger.
¹¹ The more the words,
    the less the meaning,
    and how does that profit anyone?
¹² For who knows what is good for a person in life, during the few and meaningless days they pass through like a shadow? Who can tell them what will happen under the sun after they are gone?

7

¹ A good name is better than fine perfume,
    and the day of death better than the day of birth.
² It is better to go to a house of mourning
    than to go to a house of feasting,
  for death is the destiny of everyone;
    the living should take this to heart.
³ Frustration is better than laughter,
    because a sad face is good for the heart.
⁴ The heart of the wise is in the house of mourning,
    but the heart of fools is in the house of pleasure.
⁵ It is better to heed the rebuke of a wise person
    than to listen to the song of fools.
⁶ Like the crackling of thorns under the pot,
    so is the laughter of fools.
  This too is vanity!
⁷ Extortion turns a wise person into a fool,
    and a bribe corrupts the heart.
⁸ The end of a matter is better than its beginning,
    and patience is better than pride.
⁹ Do not be quickly provoked in your spirit,
    for anger resides in the lap of fools.
¹⁰ Do not say, 'Why were the old days better than these?'
    For it is not wise to ask such questions.

¹¹ Wisdom, like an inheritance, is a good thing
  and benefits those who see the sun.
¹² Wisdom is a shelter
  as money is a shelter,
 but the advantage of knowledge is this:
  Wisdom preserves those who have it.

¹³ Consider what God has done:

Who can straighten
  what he has made crooked?
¹⁴ When times are good, be happy;
  but when times are bad, consider this:
God has made the one
  as well as the other.
Therefore, no one can discover
  anything about their future.

¹⁵ In this meaningless life of mine I have seen both of these:

  the righteous perishing in their righteousness,
    and the wicked living long in their wickedness.
¹⁶ Do not be over-righteous,
    neither be overwise—
    why destroy yourself?
¹⁷ Do not be overwicked,
    and do not be a fool—
    why die before your time?
¹⁸ It is good to grasp the one
    and not let go of the other.
    Whoever fears God will come forth with both of them[16].

¹⁹ Wisdom makes one wise person more powerful
  than ten rulers in a city.
²⁰ Indeed, there is no one on earth who is righteous,
  no one who does what is right and never sins.
²¹ Do not pay attention to every word people say,
  or you may hear your servant cursing you—
²² for you know in your heart
  that many times you yourself have cursed others.

---

16. A better translation from Hebrew.

²³ All this I tested by wisdom and I said,

'*I am determined to be wise*'—
  but this was beyond me.
²⁴ Whatever exists is far off and most profound—
  who can discover it?
²⁵ So I turned my mind to understand,
    to investigate and to search out wisdom and the scheme of things
  and to understand the stupidity of wickedness
    and the madness of folly.
²⁶ I find more bitter than death
    the woman who is a snare,
  whose heart is a trap
    and whose hands are chains.
  The man who pleases God will escape her,
    but the sinner she will ensnare.

²⁷ 'Look', **SAYS THE PREACHER (QOHELET)**, 'this is what I have discovered:
  'Adding one thing to another to discover the scheme of things—
²⁸   while I was still searching
      but not finding—
  I found one upright man among a thousand,
    but not one upright woman among them all.
²⁹ "Behold",[17] this only have I found:
    God created mankind upright,
    but they have gone in search of many schemes.'

8

¹ Who is like the wise?
  Who knows the explanation of things?
A person's wisdom brightens the face
  and changes its hard appearance.
² Obey the king's command, I say, because you took an oath before God.
³ Do not be in a hurry to leave the king's presence. Do not stand up for a bad cause, for he will do whatever he pleases. ⁴ Since a king's word is supreme, who can say to him, 'What are you doing?'

⁵ Whoever obeys his command will come to no harm,
  and the wise heart will know the proper time and procedure.

---

17. 'Behold/See', untranslated in NIV.

⁶ For there is a proper time and procedure for every matter,
   though a person may be weighed down by misery.
⁷ Since no one knows the future,
   who can tell someone else what is to come?
⁸ As no one has power over the wind to contain it,
   so no one has power over the time of their death.
  As no one is discharged in time of war,
   so wickedness will not release those who practice it.

⁹ All this I saw, as I applied my mind to everything done under the sun. There is a time when people lord it over others to their own hurt. ¹⁰ Then I saw the wicked buried. They used to come and go from the holy place! But those were forgotten in the city who had acted justly. This also is meaningless.[18]

¹¹ When the sentence for a crime is not quickly carried out, people's hearts are filled with schemes to do wrong. ¹² Although a wicked person who commits a hundred crimes may live a long time, I know that it will go better with those who fear God, who are reverent before him. ¹³ Yet because the wicked do not fear God, it will not go well with them, and their days will not lengthen like a shadow.

¹⁴ There is something else vain that occurs on earth: the righteous who get what the wicked deserve, and the wicked who get what the righteous deserve. This too, I say, is vanity. ¹⁵ So I commend the enjoyment of life, because there is nothing better for a person under the sun than to eat and drink and be glad. Then joy will accompany them in their toil all the days of the life God has given them under the sun.

¹⁶ When I applied my mind to know wisdom and to observe the labor that is done on earth—people getting no sleep day or night— ¹⁷ then I saw all that God has done. No one can comprehend what goes on under the sun. Despite all their efforts to search it out, no one can discover its meaning. Even if the wise claim they know, they cannot really comprehend it.

9

¹ Indeed[19], all this I took to my heart even to examine all this:[20] The righteous and the wise and what they do are in God's hands, but no one knows whether love or hate awaits them. ² All share a common destiny—the right-

---

18. I follow Roland Murphy's translation of this difficult verse (Murphy 1992: 79).
19. A more forceful translation.
20. A literal translation.

eous and the wicked, the good and the bad, the clean and the unclean, those who offer sacrifices and those who do not.

> As it is with the good,
>> so with the sinful;
> as it is with those who take oaths,
>> so with those who are afraid to take them.

³ This is the evil in everything that happens under the sun: The same destiny overtakes all. The hearts of people, moreover, are full of evil and there is madness in their hearts while they live, and afterward they join the dead. ⁴ Anyone who is among the living has hope—even a live dog is better off than a dead lion!

⁵ For the living know that they will die,
>> but the dead know nothing;
> they have no further reward,
>> and even their name is forgotten[21].
⁶ Their love, their hate
>> and their jealousy have long since vanished;
> never again will they have a part
>> in anything that happens under the sun.

⁷ Go, eat your food with gladness, and drink your wine with a joyful heart, for God has already approved what you do. ⁸ Always be clothed in white, and always anoint your head with oil. ⁹ Enjoy life with your wife, whom you love, all the days of your life of vanity[22] that God has given you under the sun—all your meaningless days/days of vanity.[23] For this is your lot in life and in your toilsome labor under the sun. ¹⁰ Whatever your hand finds to do, do it with all your might, for in the realm of the dead, where you are going, there is neither working nor planning nor knowledge nor wisdom.

¹¹ I returned and saw[24] under the sun:

> The race is not to the swift
>> or the battle to the strong,
> nor does food come to the wise

---

21. Literally, 'for their memory is forgotten'.
22. Literally, 'life of vanity'.
23. Literally, 'days of vanity'.
24. Literally, 'I returned and saw...', with the focus on a 180-degree 'turning'.

>   or wealth to the brilliant
>   or favor to the learned;
>   but time and chance happen to them all.

¹² Moreover, no one knows when their hour will come:

>   As fish are caught in a cruel net,
>   or birds are taken in a snare,
>   so people are trapped by evil times
>   that fall unexpectedly upon them.

¹³ I also saw under the sun this example of wisdom that greatly impressed me: ¹⁴ There was once a small city with only a few people in it. And a powerful king came against it, surrounded it and built huge siege works against it. ¹⁵ Now there lived in that city a man poor but wise, and he saved the city by his wisdom. But nobody remembered that poor man. ¹⁶ *So I said, 'Wisdom is better than strength'*. But the poor man's wisdom is despised, and his words are no longer heeded.

> ¹⁷ *The quiet words of the wise are more to be heeded*
>   *than the shouts of a ruler of fools.*
> ¹⁸ *Wisdom is better than weapons of war,*
>   *but one sinner destroys much good.*

10

> ¹ *As dead flies give perfume a bad smell,*
>   *so a little folly outweighs wisdom and honor.*
> ² *The heart of the wise inclines to the right,*
>   *but the heart of the fool to the left.*
> ³ *Even as fools walk along the road,*
>   *they lack sense*
>   *and show everyone how stupid they are.*
> ⁴ *If a ruler's anger rises against you,*
>   *do not leave your post;*
>   *calmness can lay great offenses to rest.*

>   ⁵ There is an evil I have seen under the sun,
>   the sort of error that arises from a ruler:
>   ⁶ Fools are put in many high positions,
>   while the rich occupy the low ones.
>   ⁷ I have seen slaves on horseback,
>   while princes go on foot like slaves.

⁸ Whoever digs a pit may fall into it;
   whoever breaks through a wall may be bitten by a snake.
⁹ Whoever quarries stones may be injured by them;
   whoever splits logs may be endangered by them.
¹⁰ If the axe is dull
   and its edge unsharpened,
  more strength is needed,
   but skill will bring success.
¹¹ If a snake bites before it is charmed,
   the charmer receives no fee.
¹² Words from the mouth of the wise are gracious,
   but fools are consumed by their own lips.
¹³ At the beginning their words are folly;
   at the end they are wicked madness—
¹⁴   and fools multiply words.
  No one knows what is coming—
   who can tell someone else what will happen after them?
¹⁵ The toil of fools wearies them;
   they do not know the way to town.
¹⁶ Woe to the land whose king was a servant
   and whose princes feast in the morning.
¹⁷ Blessed is the land whose king is of noble birth
   and whose princes eat at a proper time—
   for strength and not for drunkenness.
¹⁸ Through laziness, the rafters sag;
   because of idle hands, the house leaks.
¹⁹ A feast is made for laughter,
   wine makes life merry,
   and money is the answer for everything.
²⁰ Do not revile the king even in your thoughts,
   or curse the rich in your bedroom,
  because a bird in the sky may carry your words,
   and a bird on the wing may report what you say.

11

¹ Ship your grain across the sea;
   after many days you may receive a return.
² Invest in seven ventures, yes, in eight;
   you do not know what disaster may come upon the land.
³ If clouds are full of water,
   they pour rain on the earth.

>   Whether a tree falls to the south or to the north,
>   in the place where it falls, there it will lie.
> 4 Whoever watches the wind will not plant;
>   whoever looks at the clouds will not reap.
> 5 As you do not know the path of the wind,
>   or how the body is formed in a mother's womb,
>   so you cannot understand the work of God,
>   the Maker of all things.
> 6 Sow your seed in the morning,
>   and at evening let your hands not be idle,
>   for you do not know which will succeed,
>   whether this or that,
>   or whether both will do equally well.
> 7 Light is sweet,
>   and it pleases the eyes to see the sun.
> 8 However many years anyone may live,
>   let them enjoy them all.
>   But let them remember the days of darkness,
>   for there will be many.
>   Everything to come is vanity.
>
> 9 You who are young, be happy while you are young,
>   and let your heart give you joy in the days of your youth.
>   Follow the ways of your heart
>   and whatever your eyes see,
>   but know that for all these things
>   God will bring you into judgment.
> 10 So then, banish anxiety from your heart
>   and cast off the troubles of your body,
>   for youth and vigor are vanity.

12

> 1 Remember your Creator
>   in the days of your youth,
>   before the days of trouble come
>   and the years approach when you will say,
>   'I find no pleasure in them'—
> 2 before the sun and the light
>   and the moon and the stars grow dark,
>   and the clouds return after the rain;
> 3 when the keepers of the house tremble,

    and the strong men stoop,
  when the grinders cease because they are few,
    and those looking through the windows grow dim;
⁴ *when the doors to the street are closed*
    and the sound of grinding fades;
  when people rise up at the sound of birds,
    but all their songs grow faint;
⁵ *when people are afraid of heights*
    and of dangers in the streets;
  when the almond tree blossoms
    and the grasshopper drags itself along
    and desire no longer is stirred.
  Then people go to their eternal home
    and mourners go about the streets.

⁶ *Remember him—before the silver cord is severed,*
    and the golden bowl is broken;
  before the pitcher is shattered at the spring,
    and the wheel broken at the well,
⁷ *and the dust returns to the ground it came from,*
    and the spirit returns to God who gave it.

⁸ 'Vanity of vanities!' **SAYS THE PREACHER (QOHELET).**
    'All is vanity!'

⁹ And more than that[25] the Preacher was wise, but he also imparted knowledge to the people. He pondered and searched out and set in order many proverbs. ¹⁰ The Preacher searched to find just the right words, and what he wrote was upright and true.

¹¹ The words of the wise are like goads, their collected sayings like firmly embedded nails—given by one shepherd. ¹² And more than these[26], my son, be warned—

Of making many books there is no end, and much study wearies the body.

¹³ **Now all has been heard;**
    here is the conclusion of the matter:

    25. In accordance with the Hebrew text.
    26. In accordance with the Hebrew text.

**Fear God and keep his commandments,
for this is the duty of all humanity.
¹⁴ For God will bring every deed into judgment,
including every hidden thing,
whether it is good or evil.**

Commentary

(*For the text cited in this section, please refer to the 'Legend' in the 'Text and Analysis of Speaking Voices' section.*)

Interpreting the Bible is an arduous task, especially when we are dealing with a complex book like Ecclesiastes. Since the turn of the century, with the empowerment of the reader engaging in the meaning-making process, ten readers of Ecclesiastes will potentially come up with ten different interpretations of the same text. However, a few commonly accepted concepts are guiding the interpretation of any given book of the Bible. *First* is the practice of a 'text-anchored and reader-oriented' approach. The dynamics exhibited in this approach are best articulated by the term Grant R. Osborne has coined—the 'Hermeneutical Spiral' (i.e. from the horizon of the text to the horizon of the reader in a continuous and cross-enriching fashion [Osborne 1991: 6-7]). As a fitting metaphor, 'spiral' signifies a momentum that is not going round and round in a closed circle but an *open-ended* progressive, spiralling upward movement, drawing closer and closer to the intended meaning of the text. *Second,* meaning through genre is a sound interpretive principle. The primary genres of Ecclesiastes (e.g. reflection, narrative, wisdom sayings, instruction, etc.) as well as its various literary devices (e.g. poem, rhetorical questions, *carpe diem* sayings, etc.) would serve as parameters for interpretation. *Third,* the outcome of one's interpretation is toward 'appropriation' (i.e. from the meaning of the text to the contextual significance of the reader). I will seek to provide 'pointers' and 'directives' for meaning and significance in each of the major sections outlined in this commentary.

Affirming the above-stated notions, I shall undertake a three-world approach in this commentary. A three-world approach to interpretation entails paying due attention to the *world behind the text,* the *world of the text* and the *world in front of the text.* Due to the lack of direct historical reference in the book, I shall undertake a 'historically inquiring synchronic reading (i.e. reading with time vs. reading through time = diachronic reading'; see Steck 2000: 20). My focus will be on both the 'textual world' and the 'readerly world' (i.e. readers' engagement in the meaning-making process as they put themselves in front of the world of the text). After all, meaning-making comes at the intersection between text and reader.

Perspectives elucidated in the 'Approaching Ecclesiastes: Reading Strategies' section above (namely, reading narratively, reading polyphonically, reading dialectically, reading 'cross the grains', and reading as a memoir) will collectively play a major role here, providing 'points of entry' to respective passages. Given that Ecclesiastes is a multivoiced book, readers are encouraged to 'hear the text' (or to practise the 'hermeneutics of hearing') toward interpretation. This is done through dialoguing with the other voices engrained in the twelve chapters, to shape and construct our own interpretive voice.

The lack of coherence has been a commonly recognized challenge in reading Ecclesiastes. Various attempts have been made to come up with a logical division of the different sections of the book. Yet, success in reaching a well-received structure representing the train of thought amidst the apparent fragmented portions within the book escapes us. Shaped by the vision and objective of respective commentary series, commentators approach the interpretation with a preset intention for their target audience. From the past decades till the most current interpretive scene, structural analyses of the book can generally be classified under four trajectories. *First* is to divide the book into three broad, logical sections (Introduction [1.1-11]; Reflections/body of the book [1.12–12.8]; and Epilogue [12.9-14]). While using 'reflections' of Qohelet as the central theme, these attempts give readers the impression that within the body of the book (i.e. 1.12–12.8), there is no intentional sequence to tie the units together, and each of the three sections can stand on its own (cf. Crenshaw 1987: 5-6, 34-49; Longman 1998: 22). *Second* are those attempts that use a detailed literary analysis (e.g. reflection, wisdom instruction), linguistic and syntactic markers (e.g. Walton 2006) to analyze the main body of the book. These efforts indicate, on the one hand, the prominent themes within the book. On the other hand, they represent a resistance toward oversimplification (cf. Enns 2011: 22-27; Longman 1998: 22). Designating 'reflections' as the main genre with the identification of several varia ('varied unconnected topics') represents the *third* approach. They allow the topics (or varia) to stand on their own as they come naturally in the book (e.g. Weeks 2020, 2021; Murphy 1992). Among this group, Choon-Leong Seow (1997) provides a creative structure for the main body ('Reflection [1.2–6.9]—Ethics [5.1–6.9/MT 5.7–6.9])—Reflection [6.10–8.17]—Ethics [9.1–12.8]'). It demonstrates a more intentional effort to connect the main sections in terms of 'reflection' and 'ethics' but fails to demonstrate the natural flow of thought or textual continuity within (see esp. Seow 1997: 46-47). Thomas

Krüger (2004) stands alone in his rationale regarding the *hebel* in 1.2-3 as essentially a critique. Rooted in the wisdom tradition, he proposed a structural outline that is characterized by a combination of critique of the king/wise man, exhortations, as well as the limit of wisdom/wise man. As a unique and perhaps less coarse outline, it undermines primarily the power of the individual 'I'-voice of Qohelet, as well as the dialogic dynamics of other voices in this polyphonic book.

The *fourth* trajectory is the most original, innovative and illuminating one, and is represented by John Goldingay (see his own evaluation, Goldingay 2021a: 57) and Knut Heim (2019). Using the fundamental conviction about life ('everything is a mere breath' [1.2]), Goldingay puts the third-person narrator (1.1; 12.9-14) in the foreground and accepts that there is no explainable rationale behind the order of the main body. He has proposed an interpretive outline that is theologically sound (2021a: 56-57). Heim's recent commentary offers the most impactful and sensible structural analysis, which is composed of eleven 'case studies' and five 'practical interludes' (practical instructions) interwoven with several reflections and instructions. In distinction from the traditional approach to the commentary proper, Heim delivers an interpretive thrust that is rooted in the collective flesh-and-blood lived experience of today's readers (i.e. the 'Grand Narrative').

Distinct from the worked-out proposals by scholars in the recent past, I present here an analytical outline that foregrounds the five dialogic voices embedded in the text (see discussion in 'Text and Analysis of Speaking Voices' section). It represents my vigorous efforts in coming up with an integrated reading strategy in keeping with the nature of the book. My take on whether Ecclesiastes is essentially a pessimistic or optimistic book (or something other than this polar concept) will naturally shape my interpretation. The demand for readers to practise 'hearing the text' is another interpretive goal. I would encourage all readers walking this interpretive path not only to follow the outline but 'to practise' with a high level of self-engagement, dialoging with the different voices ingrained in the text with your own interpretive voice. Not only is it a demonstration of 'how' the proposed interpretive strategies shape our practice; more so, it is an interpretive exercise reinforcing our strategies of reading. Notwithstanding its imperfection, I seek to offer here a more comprehensive, sensible and non-fragmented outline, demonstrating the trajectory of the flow of thoughts represented by the vital-dialogic dynamics within this polyphonic book.

Using voice analysis as an overarching framework, the interpretive outline presented below is highlighted with the five voices represented in Ecclesiastes: the voice of the frame narrator, Qohelet's first-person voice, Qohelet's inner voice, the collective voice of wisdom, and the voice of the epilogist.

A. Third-person frame narrator introducing Qohelet and the fundamental conviction: 'Vanity of vanities! All is vanity!' (1.1-3)

B. Second-person collective voice of wisdom spelling out the conviction of God's order of creation and the order of God's ruling (1.4-11)

C. Qohelet's first-person voice reflecting on his *personal life experience* (in dialogue with his **inner voice**) (1.12–2.26)
   1. First personal experience (1.12-18)
      Reflective summary: 'And behold, all is vanity, a chasing after the wind!' (1.14)
      'This, too, is a chasing after the wind!' (1.17)
   2. Second personal experience (2.1-11)
      Reflective summary: 'And behold, this also is vanity!' (2.1)
      'And behold, all was vanity and a chasing after the wind!' (2.11)
   3. Third personal experience (2.12-23)
      Reflective summary: 'All is vanity, a chasing after the wind!' (2.17)
      'This too is vanity!' (2.23)
   4. First *carpe diem* saying (2.24-26)
      Reflective summary: 'This too is vanity, a chasing after the wind!' (2.26)

D. Second-person voice of wisdom affirming God's order of things (3.1-15)
   1. There is a time for everything (3.1-11)
   2. Second *carpe diem* saying (3.12-13) and the ending (3.14-15)

E. Qohelet's first-person voice reflecting on his *exploration of life* in dialogue with his **inner voice** (3.16–4.16)
   1. First cycle of exploration (3.16-21)
   2. Third *carpe diem* saying (3.22)
   3. Second cycle of exploration (4.1-3)
   4. Third cycle of exploration (4.4)
      Interlude: **Second-person wisdom sayings** (4.5-6)
   5. Fourth cycle of exploration (4.7-16)
      Interlude: **Second-person wisdom sayings** (4.9-14)
      Reflective summary: 'This too is vanity, a chasing after the wind!' (4.15-16)

F. **Second-person wisdom's instruction** on 'Fearing God' (5.1-7 [MT 4.17–5.6])
   > Interlude: **Second-person wisdom sayings** (5.8-12 [MT 5.7-11])

G. **Qohelet's first-person** *exploration of life* continued (5.13–6.12 [MT 5.12–6.12])
   1. Fifth cycle of exploration (5.13-17 [MT 5.12-16])
   2. Fourth *carpe diem* saying (5.18-20 [MT 5.17-19])
   3. Sixth cycle of exploration (6.1-12)

H. **Second-person wisdom sayings** (7.1-14)
   1. 'Better than' sayings (7.1-12)
   2. Wisdom's voice affirming the order of God's ruling (7.12-13)

I. **Qohelet's first-person** *exploration of life* continued (7.15–10.7)
   1. Seventh cycle of exploration (7.15-18)
      > Interlude: **Second-person wisdom sayings** (7.19-22)
   2. Eighth cycle of exploration (7.23-26)
   3. Ninth cycle of exploration (7.27–8.8)
      > Interlude: **Second-person wisdom sayings** (8.1-8)
   4. Tenth cycle of exploration (8.9-13)
      Reflective summary: on fearing God (8.12-13)
   5. Eleventh cycle of exploration (8.14)
   6. Fifth *carpe diem* saying (8.15)
   7. Twelfth cycle of exploration (8.16-17)
   8. Thirteenth cycle of exploration (9.1-2)
   9. Fourteenth cycle of exploration (9.3-6)
   10. Sixth *carpe diem* saying (9.7-10)
   11. Fifteenth cycle of exploration (9.11-12)
   12. Sixteenth cycle of exploration (9.13-16)
       > Interlude: **Second-person wisdom sayings** (9.17–10.4)
   13. Seventeenth cycle of exploration (10.5-7)

J. **Second-person wisdom sayings** (10.8-12.7)
   1. Wisdom is indeed better than folly: The strength and limits of wisdom (10.8-20)
   2. Advice for life in view of the uncertainties of the risky future (11.1-8)
   3. Seventh *carpe diem* saying (11.9-10)
   4. Live life fully in the 'present' and aware of the certainty of bad times: 'Remember your Creator!' (12.1-7)

K. **Qohelet's first-person** summary appraisal, echoing the fundamental conviction: 'Vanity of vanities! All is vanity!' (12.8)

L. **Voice of the epilogist** responding to Qohelet's fundamental conviction about life: 'Vanity of vanities! All is vanity!' (12.9-14)

* * *

A. **Third-Person Frame Narrator Introducing Qohelet and the Fundamental Conviction: 'Vanity of Vanities! All is Vanity!' (1.1-3)**

1

¹ THE WORDS OF THE PREACHER (QOHELET[1]). SON OF DAVID, KING IN JERUSALEM:
² 'Vanity of vanities!'[2]
    SAYS QOHELET.
'Vanity of vanities!
    All is vanity!'
³ What do people gain from all their labors
    at which they toil under the sun?

The third-person narrator provides a framing for Ecclesiastes to be read narratively in 1.1-3. Qohelet is the primary speaker in the book (for discussion on the translation of the Hebrew word *Qohelet*, see Krüger 2004: 11; Goldingay 2021: 58), and this designation will be used in this commentary as the preacher who always speaks in the first-person 'I'-voice. He is introduced to readers as a person of royalty—the son of David, king in Jerusalem (1.1). Commentators generally agree that the anonymity of this preacher is intentional. The focus in the depiction (vv. 1-2) is that Qohelet was once leading a royal life and endowed with wisdom like that of Solomon. This is in accordance with the wisdom tradition designating Solomon as a wise man.

Qohelet's first words—'Vanity of vanities, all is vanity!' (literally, 'mere breath, a mere breath' is a hyperbole like 'utterly absurd' or 'vanity of vanities; all is vanity' is another hyperbole) sets the tone for the whole

---

1. 'Qohelet' is the transliteration of the Hebrew word which bears the root meaning of 'one who convenes an assembly'. Qohelet/the preacher represents the primary 'I'-speaking voice in the book. The Hebrew word 'Qohelet' is used in this commentary to distinguish it from the name of the book of Ecclesiastes.

2. My preferred translation of the Hebrew word (*hbl*) is 'vanity' instead of 'meaningless'.

book. Fox notes, 'vanity of vanities, all is vanity' is a *protest* against God (Fox 1999: 49; see also Krüger 2004: 42-44). Qohelet is protesting to God that all he has experienced under the sun is utterly absurd, meaningless (1.2)! This is an anguished cry directed to God. Reading Ecclesiastes as Qohelet's memoir would help readers to appreciate that Qohelet needs an effective literary vehicle, a platform to carry his overwhelming, distressed feelings. Verse 3 can be understood in at least in two ways. *First,* serving as an important introduction to the whole book, v. 3 underscores an 'inquiring spirit' in Qohelet's narration—'What would people gain from all their labors at which they toil under the sun?' *Second,* if this probing question is read as merely his rhetoric, then it serves a dual purpose. (1) It enforces Qohelet's *dispute* with God. (2) As a 'first-person projection of a third-person view', this rhetorical question positions the query against the collective human experience under the sun. It is not prompted by the successful royal figure Qohelet's personal life experience as self-narrated in 1.12–2.26, but an outcry of all humanity who share the same reality in life ('what *gain* ... their *labor* ... they *toil* under the sun'). It thus broadens and deepens the cluster of emotive feelings embedded in v. 3, and readers are being called upon to listen to the depth of Qohelet's/humanity's outcry and respond emotively. For Qohelet's readers/audience, the invitation to 'hearing the text' is in effect at the beginning of the book. Although it is a matter of foregrounding, my reading leads toward the latter signification.

B. Second-Person Collective Voice of Wisdom Spelling out the Order of God's Creation and the Order of God's Ruling (1.4-11)

⁴ Generations come and generations go,
    but the earth remains forever.
⁵ The sun rises and the sun sets,
    and hurries back to where it rises.
⁶ The wind blows to the south
    and turns to the north;
round and round it goes,
    ever returning on its course.
⁷ All streams flow into the sea,
    yet the sea is never full.
To the place the streams come from,
    there they return again.
⁸ All things are wearisome,
    more than one can say.

> *The eye never has enough of seeing,*
> *nor the ear its fill of hearing.*
> ⁹ *What has been will be again,*
> *what has been done will be done again;*
> *there is nothing new under the sun.*
> ¹⁰ *Is there anything of which one can say,*
> *'Look! This is something new'?*
> *It was here already, long ago;*
> *it was here before our time.*
> ¹¹ *No one remembers the former generations,*
> *and even those yet to come*
> *will not be remembered*
> *by those who follow them.*

Ecclesiastes is wisdom literature. As wisdom literature, it shares a pivotal theme with the other wisdom books: 'the order of things'. While, on the one hand, Proverbs affirms God's order of ruling in human lives in keeping with the so-called blessing-and-cursing principle (Prov. 3.33), Job, on the other hand, laments silently the apparent unjust order of God's ruling ('How often would the lamp of the wicked be snuffed out?', Job 21.17). Yet, Job submits to God's sovereignty at the end, after God spoke to him out of the whirlwind (Job 38–39). Here in Ecclesiastes, the second-person wisdom's voice emerges in 1.4-11, affirming both God's order of creation (vv. 4-7) and God's order of ruling in human lives (vv. 8-11) through the literary medium of a poem. Out of the vanities of humanity's experience under the sun, this poetry boldly pronounces the conviction that though generations come and go, one stability remains forever—'God's order of things' (i.e. what is happening in the universe and what is going to happen to humanity on earth). On the one hand, it opens a forum for the answer to the two rhetorical questions in v. 3 ('What would people gain from all their labors at which they toil under the sun?') and v. 10 ('Is there anything of which one can say, "Look! This is something new"?'). On the other hand, it presents a sharp contrast between the steady consistency of the cosmos going about its cyclical way in accordance with God's created order and the frustrated repetitiveness of humanity's experience under the sun, which goes nowhere (Goldingay 2021:75). The poem further spells out God's created order—the rising and setting of the sun (v. 5); the set path of the blowing wind and returning to its course (v. 6); and the never-filling sea with the torrents always going back (v. 7). It paints a picture of the constants in God's created order, such as the circuits of sun, wind and water show; and the constants of human existence (summed up in the reflective expression—'All things are wearisome', v. 8).

Reading 1.4-11 from this perspective, the articulation of the cosmic and human activities on earth can be presented in the following analysis. It indicates the trajectory of the eight sets of depiction from 'cosmic and human activities' to 'constants/norms':

Cosmic and Human Activities	→	Constants/Norms
(1) A generation comes, and a generation goes, (1.4)		But the earth remains forever.
(2) The sun rises and the sun sets, and hurries to where it rises (1.5).		It rises there again.
(3) The wind blows to the south and turns to the north: round and round it goes (1.6).		Ever returning on its course.
(4) All streams flow into the sea, yet the sea is never full. To the place the streams come from (1.7).		There they return (again).
(5) The eye never has enough of seeing, nor the ear its fill of hearing (1.8).		All things are worrisome.
(6) What has been will be again, what has been done has been done again (1.9).		There is nothing new under the sun.
(7) Is there anything of which one can say, 'Look! This is something new'? It was there already, long ago … (1.10).		There is nothing new under the sun.
(8) No one remembers the former generations. And even those yet to come will not be remembered by those who follow them (1.11).		There is nothing new under the sun.

While classical theory sees poetry as the imitation of reality, the emotion theory construes it as the spontaneous outpouring of powerful feelings (Petersen and Richards 1992: 12). This poem sets the stage for Qohelet's prevailing emotive response in vv. 8-11. Though eyes and ears have never had enough of seeing and hearing things *new*, the sum of humanity's experience through seeing and hearing is 'wearisome' (v. 8). The various aspects of the same 'constant' is explicated in vv. 9-11. In a more emphatic manner, vv. 9-10 points to the unchangeable(s) in God's order of ruling—'There is nothing new under the sun' (v. 9) and supplemented with a more affective rhetorical question: 'Is there anything of which one can say, "Look! This is something new"?' (v. 10). This question is reinforced by the answer 'it was here already, long ago; it was here before our time' (v. 10). The residue of the meaninglessness and absurdity of human life is found at the end of the poem, breaking the human search for some continuity in this 'Grand Narrative'—'No one remembers the former generations, and even those yet to come will not be remembered by those who follow them' (v. 11).

The analysis above helps readers to follow the flow of Qohelet's thoughts and emotive response. It moves from upholding the conviction of God's created order, the normative universal truths, on to humanity's emotive response under God's ruling in our lives in God's created world. In doing so, the affirmation that God is the Creator God looms large yet without undermining the distressed feeling of humanity's experience under the sun (v. 8). This is done through the literary medium of a poem. Humanity cannot change the constants, but human responses are the variables. This first passage sets the background for our understanding of the following chapters and opens new opportunities for variables in our readerly response! Therefore, be engaged.

C. Qohelet's First-Person Voice Reflecting on his 'Personal' Life Experience (in Dialogue with his 'Inner Voice') (1.12–2.26)

1. First personal experience (1.12-18)
Reflective summary: 'And behold! All is vanity, a chasing after the wind!' (1.14)
'This too, is a chasing after the wind!' (1.17)

[12] I, the Teacher, was king over Israel in Jerusalem. [13] I applied my heart[3] to study and to explore by wisdom all that is done under the heavens. What a heavy burden God has laid on humanity! [14] I have seen all the things that are done under the sun; and behold[4], all is vanity, a chasing after the wind.

[15] What is crooked cannot be straightened;
   what is lacking cannot be counted.

[16] *I said in my heart[5], 'Behold, I have increased in wisdom more than anyone who has ruled over Jerusalem before me; I have experienced much of wisdom and knowledge'.* [17] Then I applied myself to the understanding of wisdom, and also of madness and folly, but I learned that this, too, is a chasing after the wind.

---

3. The Hebrew word used is 'heart'.
4. 'And behold' represents the captivating force in the Hebrew text, left untranslated in NIV.
5. Literally, 'I spoke with my heart'.

¹⁸ For with much wisdom comes much sorrow;
   the more knowledge, the more grief.

In an emphatic, self-referential 'I, the Qohelet', Qohelet begins his reflection on his personal life experience (v. 12). First, he affirms his royal status as king over Israel in Jerusalem (v. 12). The level of his engagement in this search is articulated as 'I gave my heart', and the path is by 'wisdom' (v. 13). It is interesting to note that both thought and emotion are attributed to the 'heart' (see North 1993: 592-97). The manner of his search is presented as personal eyewitness ('I have seen'), and the scope of his search—'all which is done under the heavens' (referring to the collective *human experience* under the sun). The depiction here points to an all flesh-and-blood *personal* experience, the engagement of the whole self. He comes to realize that this is an evil task that God has given to humankind (v. 13). Qohelet then comes to an emphatic reflective summary: 'And behold! All is vanity, a chasing after the wind' (v. 14). This reflection is followed by another affirmation of the order of God's ruling, 'what is crooked cannot be straightened; what is lacking cannot be counted' (v. 15).

Verse 16 introduces the third voice in Ecclesiastes, Qohelet's 'inner voice'. *First,* it is done by dividing himself up into two halves ('I said in my heart': i.e. his internal self and his external self) to create a space for himself to dialogue/debate with his 'inner self'. As pioneers in the field of speaking voice analysis, Meir Sternberg and Alonso Schökel have been successful in exemplifying 'monologue-dialogue' in the Hebrew Bible. Contained within the pericope are pockets of monologues within dialogue and imaginary dialogues within monologue (Sternberg 1986: 295-318; Alonso Schökel 1998). One can therefore collapse the distinctiveness between monologue and dialogue as they serve the same function of 'self-representation'. *Second,* in Qohelet's interior dialogue, he begins with 'behold' (v. 16) and expands his dialogic reflection through self-examining his own accomplishments through the path guided by wisdom and experiential knowledge ('Behold, I have increased in wisdom more than anyone who has ruled over Jerusalem before me; I have experienced wisdom and knowledge' [v. 17]). As Adele Berlin has noted, 'behold' here functions as an 'interior monologue', an internalized viewpoint that provides an 'interior vision' (Berlin 1994: 62-63). In his personal reflection, Qohelet is saying to his inner self, I daringly tried it out through walking the two paths that are of polar contrast: that of wisdom and of madness and folly (v. 17). In an enclosed structure, his reflective summary here echoes the same reflective summary in v. 14—'This too, is a chasing after the wind'. Reading Ecclesiastes narratively, our interpretation is always set against the background of the flesh-and-blood lived experience of humanity under the sun. The summary of this first *personal* experience presents yet another paradoxical notion: the negative side of wisdom and knowledge—'For with much wisdom comes much sorrow; the more knowledge, the more grief' (v. 18). Reading Ecclesiastes dialectically and polyphonically helps to uncover the literary dynamics contained in Qohelet's first *personal* and experiential reflection.

2. Second personal experience (2.1-11)
Reflective summary: 'And behold, this also is vanity!' (2.1)
'And behold, all was vanity and a chasing after the wind!' (2.11)

2
I said to my heart, 'Come now, I will test you with pleasure to find out what is good'. But behold, this too is vanity. ² 'Laughter', I said, 'is madness. And what does pleasure accomplish?' ³I tried cheering myself with wine and embracing folly—my mind still guiding me with wisdom. I wanted to see what was good for people to do under the heavens during the few days of their lives.

⁴I undertook great projects: I built houses for myself and planted vineyards. ⁵I made gardens and parks and planted all kinds of fruit trees in them. ⁶I made reservoirs to water groves of flourishing trees. ⁷I bought male and female slaves and had other slaves who were born in my house. I also owned more herds and flocks than anyone in Jerusalem before me. ⁸I amassed silver and gold for myself, and the treasure of kings and provinces. I acquired male and female singers, and a harem as well—the delights of a man's heart. ⁹I became greater by far than anyone in Jerusalem before me. In all this my wisdom stayed with me.

¹⁰ I denied myself nothing my eyes desired;
  I refused my heart no pleasure.
 My heart took delight in all my labor,
  and this was the reward for all my toil.
¹¹ Yet when I surveyed all that my hands had done
  and what I had toiled to achieve,
 and behold, all was vanity, a chasing after the wind;
  nothing was gained under the sun.

In an enclosed structure, this episode begins and ends with the motto of the book, 'All is vanity and a chasing after the wind' (vv. 1, 11). Both places are highlighted with an emphatic interior monologue, 'behold', signifying an astonishing realization after Qohelet's personal lived experience. Verse 1 begins with an interior monologue (or a dialogue between Qohelet and his inner self), indicating Qohelet's determination to conduct an experiment in pursuing pleasure and goodness (v. 2), and this pursuit is 'self-embracing' ('to lay hold on', v. 2). As Roland Murphy has noted, 'till I might *see* what is good' (v. 3, literally the Hebrew reads, 'and look upon good'). The Hebrew verb 'see' here carries the nuance of 'experience, partake of' (Murphy 1992: 16 n. 1a; cf. 2.24; 3.13; 9.9; Job 9.25; Ps. 34.9 [MT 34.8]). The expression points to the determined goal of his exploration: 'to see what was good for people to do under the heavens during the few days of their life'. One conviction stands out in v. 3 (also echoed in v. 9): 'My heart still guiding me with wisdom'. Verse 3 presents a case in point, in that amidst the expression of distressed feelings, Qohelet never stops reminding his audience of his convictions (let it be the value of wisdom, faith in God's order of ruling in human lives, and the importance of the fear of God and worship, etc.).

Verses 4-11 are action oriented. 'I built, I planted, I made, I brought, I owned, I gathered ...'. All are attributed to the great projects Qohelet has undertaken. They cover spheres of the community, Qohelet's household, and personal wealth and pleasure. His wealth is like the treasure owned by the kings, and his pleasure is fulfilling the delights of a man's heart (vv. 7-8). Verse 9b, 'In all this my wisdom stayed with me', underscores a theme in this episode—all his pleasure-seeking and accomplishments are guided by wisdom (vv. 3, 9b). Verse 10 apparently gives answer to the question posed in 1.3—'What do people gain from all their labors at which they toil under the sun?' In that he was saying to himself, 'my heart took delight in all my labor, and that was the reward for all my toil'. Yet in another emphatic interior monologue ('behold!'), Qohelet concludes that all his achievements and toils were vanities, just like a chasing after the wind; nothing was gained under the sun (v. 11). This reflective summary echoes the motto of the book and forms an enclosure in this episode (vv. 1, 11). Reading Ecclesiastes dialectically, this kind of sudden twist is to be expected, and it is to be perceived as part of Qohelet's lived experience under the sun.

3. Third personal experience (2.12-23)
Reflective summary: 'This too is vanity!' (2.15, 23)
   'All is vanity, a chasing after the wind!'
   (2.17, 26)

[12] Then I turned my thoughts to consider wisdom,
   and also madness and folly.
What more can the king's successor do
   than what has already been done?
[13] I saw that wisdom is better than folly,
   just as light is better than darkness.

¹⁴ The wise have eyes in their heads,
  while the fool walks in the darkness;
 but I came to realize
  that the same fate overtakes them both.

¹⁵ Then I said to myself,
 'The fate of the fool will overtake me also.
  What then do I gain by being wise?'
 I said to myself,
  'This too is meaningless'.
¹⁶ For the wise, like the fool, will not be long remembered;
  the days have already come when both have been forgotten.
 And how does the wise die like the fool⁶!

¹⁷ So I hated life, because the work that is done under the sun was grievous to me. All is vanity, a chasing after the wind. ¹⁸ I hated all the things I had toiled for under the sun, because I must leave them to the one who comes after me. ¹⁹ And who knows whether that person will be wise or foolish? Yet they will have control over all the fruit of my toil into which I have poured my effort and skill under the sun. This too is vanity. ²⁰ So my heart began to despair over all my toilsome labor under the sun. ²¹ For a person may labor with wisdom, knowledge, and skill, and then they must leave all they own to another who has not toiled for it. This too is vanity and a great misfortune. ²² What do people get for all the toil and anxious striving with which they labor under the sun? ²³ All their days their work is grief and pain; even at night their minds do not rest. This too is vanity.

This section of Qohelet's focused experiment on embracing wisdom and folly (vv. 12-16) is marked with a splendid sonata of literary features: (1) two interior dialogues with his own heart (v. 15); (2) four rhetorical questions to highlight his frustration and the emotional impact upon him of his searching (vv. 12, 15, 19, 22); (3) an intense emotive response (vv. 17-26); and (4) six anguished outcries ('All is vanity, a chasing after the wind!', vv. 15, 17, 19, 21, 23, 26). 'I turned to see wisdom' (literally, 'I faced to see/explore wisdom', v. 12) points to a new direction of his experiment. Taking on the persona of King Solomon, he wanted to know what will a man do after the king who has embraced wisdom, madness and folly (like what the king has done)? He came to realize that wisdom is better than folly, just as light is better than darkness (v. 13). The following verses present the first startling irony in the book. A contrast picture

  6. Literally, the Hebrew text.

is presented here: the wise man's eyes are in his head, but the fool walks in darkness (v. 14). Though the wise and the fool pursue two different paths, yet one event overtakes all of them. The phrase 'I came to realize' (v. 14b) underscores the reality that their destiny remains the same. Verse 16b spells out precisely Qohelet's frustration, 'how does the wise die with (= just like) the fool!' This empirical realization drives Qohelet into two interior debates with his own heart (v. 15). He needs a space to dialogue internally with his inner self to resolve the contradiction: two different paths, two distinct outcomes (v. 14, see Prov. 4.18-19), but leading to the *same* destiny (v. 16; see 7.15 and 8.14). In the form of a rhetorical question, Qohelet is letting out his lament: 'The fate of the fool will overtake me also. What then do I gain by being wise?' (v. 15b). He then utters another lamenting cry, 'This too is vanity!' (v. 15b).

Qohelet's emotive response in vv. 17-25 is exemplified by four lamenting cries: 'All is vanity, this too is vanity!' (vv. 17, 19, 21, 23). They are intense and startling (esp. vv. 17-18, 23). If the function of the two interior dialogues (with his heart) is to create a space for him to come to terms with his frustrations, then the outcome is despair and pain as expressed in the four lamenting cries. They are not an impulsive outbreak of his anger, as the Chinese expression says—'*Fû xin zìwèn*' (literally, 'self-examination through dialoguing with one's own heart'); they are an intense act of self-examination. Against the context of the four lamenting cries ('all is vanity!' i.e. after looking back on his life journey of toilsome labors yielding the result of pain and desperation), then the four rhetorical questions intensify the frustration and the uncertainty he is facing ('What more can the king's successor do than what has already been done?' [v. 12]; 'The fate of the fool will overtake me also. What then do I gain by being wise?' [v. 15b]; 'And who knows whether that person will be wise or foolish?' [v. 19]; 'What do people get for all the toil and anxious striving with which they labor under the sun?' [v. 22]). After the self-engaging experiments and intense self-examination, Qohelet expressed his distress with an emphatic statement: 'Therefore I hated life, because the work that is done under the sun was grievous to me ... I hated all things I had toiled for under the sun' (vv. 17-18). The verb 'hate' here suggests 'anger' and an exasperation related to sorrow and grief, an inner agony (Goldingay 2021a: 99-100). Fox sees that v. 17 indicates a transition of Qohelet's looking back in his life, and for a moment, he came to detest life (Fox 1999: 184).

Reading vv. 17-25 from the perspective of an episode of Qohelet's memoir, I find that the memoir genre provides the platform for the memoirist to freely express the submerged emotions through the 'I'-voice. This includes breaking his monologue into two pockets of interior dialogues. Qohelet's emotive response is thus powerfully staged in the foreground and potentially transmitted to readers in terms of emotive experiencing.

4. First *carpe diem* saying (2.24-26)
Reflective summary: 'This too is vanity, a chasing after the wind!' (2.26)

²⁴ A person can do nothing better than to eat and drink and find satisfaction in their own toil. This too, I see, is from the hand of God, ²⁵ for without him, who can eat or find enjoyment? ²⁶ To the person who pleases him, God gives wisdom, knowledge, and happiness, but to the sinner he gives the task of gathering and storing up wealth to hand it over to the one who pleases God. This too is vanity, a chasing after the wind.

Chapter 2 ends with a surprising twist. Verses 24-26 present the first of the seven so-called *carpe diem* ('seize the day') sayings (or the 'joy passages'). William Brown sees it as a modestly upbeat notion that serves as a conclusion of Qohelet's investigation in 1.12–2.26 (Brown 2000: 37). The insertion of these joy passages amid the outcries of 'vanity' has generated a host of scholarly debate. At one end of the spectrum, Whybray notes that Qohelet presents a gospel of joy here. Enjoyment is what enables a person to transcend the burdensome realities of human existence (Whybray 1989: 91). At the opposite end, Fox notes that this endorsement of enjoyment in life can only be found meaningful in a crazy person's private world (Fox 1999: 130). He notes that v. 26 denotes an asymmetry of efforts, and Qohelet finds this absurdity offensive. It is based on a psychological mechanism in which the sense of guilt provokes the sufferer. Subsequently, Qohelet identifies himself as the sinner in v. 26, regardless of what he has done (Fox 1999: 191). James Crenshaw presents a middle-ground view. Since life is profitless, totally absurd, therefore enjoy life if you can and even as you enjoy, know that the world is still meaningless (Crenshaw 1987: 23). More recently, Mark Boda takes their function as affirming the bodiliness of creaturely life and making the best out of the situation is the key (2013: 257-82). John Kessler sees the seven as 'theological compromise' in such a pessimistic book (2013: 275). These middle-ground perspectives have somehow marginalized the significance of the seven *carpe diem* sayings from the core message of Ecclesiastes.

Eunny Lee's monograph points out two important observations on the *carpe diem* sayings. *First*, the focus of our reading should be placed on the significant insertions of these joy passages if Ecclesiastes is to be read as a unified composition. *Second*, the *carpe diem* sayings appear sporadically through the twelve chapters. As a *connective* device, we should look at them from the perspective of the ways they effectively link together in developing Qohelet's multifaceted thoughts. The insertions are part of Qohelet's rhetorical strategies, which play on ambiguity and indeterminacy of meaning to subvert traditional expectation (Lee 2005: 31). Likewise, my focus here is on the flow of thought of Qohelet's 'I'-voice narration. In the context of dire misery as elaborated emphatically in vv. 12-23, the endorsement of eating, drinking and enjoyment in life is not the issue here (v. 24). In his distress, Qohelet brings forth two affirmations: (1) All goodness and the ability to enjoy life is from the hand of God (v. 24). (2) God is the giver of all these gifts (v. 25). Embracing 'miseries' and 'enjoyment in life' are held in dialectic tension. It is through accepting both that the outcome of a 'cross-graining' reading strategy is proven as promising, yielding broadened perspectives to the reader's meaning-making. It thus opens new potential for understanding the text better—from a single dimension to a multifaceted significance about life. As Fox notes, 'Though troubled by what he sees, he (Qohelet) does not lose his equilibrium' (1999: 26).

Verse 26 could be read from two alternate perspectives. *First,* if Qohelet identifies himself as the 'sinner' in v. 26 (in the sense 'I must have done something wrong'), then he should be at ease with all his toils and labors being handed over to the one who pleases God. Yet his *personal* life experience contradicts what he affirms to his audience here (v. 26). The feeling of unfairness drives him to end this unit with the sixth lamenting cry: 'All is vanity and a chasing after wind'. *Second,* and what I believe is the most natural reading: after the double affirmations of God's order of ruling in humanity's life under the sun (see Prov. 3.33; Deut. 11.26-28), which is deeply rooted in his pretext (the traditional wisdom), Qohelet is still overwhelmed with the outpouring of negative emotions. Driven by the dire agony of his life experience, the injustice he has endured, the uncertainty he is facing, and the apparent lack of 'order' in God's ruling in human lives (i.e. the same fate overtakes the fool and the wise), he ends his reflection with the same echo: 'All is vanity, a chasing after the wind!' This reading presents an interpretive tension here. Readers are reminded that reading Ecclesiastes is not so much gearing toward resolution of tension but to find out what it means to us—the readers. Adopting a 'cross-graining' reading strategy for the book can illuminate new dimensions of meaning. Perhaps tensions are not meant to be resolved. Sustaining interpretive tensions or embracing ambiguity in meaning may provoke in us a determination to make some sense of this paradox. This indeterminacy thus opens new possibilities and invites our readerly response.

D. Second-Person Voice of Wisdom Affirming God's Order of Things (3.1-15)

1. There is a time for everything (3.1-11)

3

There is a time for everything,
* and a season for every activity under the heavens:*
² a time to be born and a time to die,
* a time to plant and a time to uproot,*
³ a time to kill and a time to heal,
* a time to tear down and a time to build,*
⁴ a time to weep and a time to laugh,
* a time to mourn and a time to dance,*
⁵ a time to scatter stones and a time to gather them,
* a time to embrace and a time to refrain from embracing,*
⁶ a time to search and a time to give up,
* a time to keep and a time to throw away,*
⁷ a time to tear and a time to mend,
* a time to be silent and a time to speak,*
⁸ a time to love and a time to hate,
* a time for war and a time for peace.*

⁹ What do workers gain from their toil? ¹⁰ I have seen the burden God has laid on humanity with which to be preoccupied[7]. ¹¹ He has made everything beautiful in its time. He has also set eternity in the human heart; yet no one can fathom what God has done from beginning to end.

The Hebrew concept of time serves as the context for our interpretation of this poem. It differs fundamentally from contemporary understanding. In the classical Hebrew mentality, 'there is no conceptual separation between an event and the time in which it occurs. Time, like the event or series of occurrences defining it, is a dynamic, phasic phenomenon' (Thienhaus 1999: 442). Time is not an abstract concept. Recognition of time is determined by the events that take place in it. In essence, time is content determined, subjectively perceived and phasic in nature.

Reading Ecclesiastes polyphonically, after Qohelet's six anguished cries in ch. 2 (vv. 15, 17, 19, 21, 23, 26), the second-person voice of wisdom joins in the dialogue in the form of a poem on time. This passage begins with the statement: 'There is a time for everything, and a season for every activity under the heavens' (v. 1). Verses 2-8 list fourteen pairs of opposites reflect-

---

7. The latter part of v. 10 remains untranslated in NIV.

ing the polar structure of the book, and they all concern human activities under the heavens. The passage contains one rhetorical question ('What do workers gain from all their toil?', v. 9), echoing the query posed in 1.3, and it concludes with the second *carpe diem* saying (vv. 12-13) in the book. As Craig Bartholomew observes, by using the verb 'know' twice (signifying experiential knowledge vs. head knowledge in Hebrew, e.g. Gen. 4.1; Hos. 11.3), the passage ends with two confessional statements (vv. 12, 14; Bartholomew 2009: 167-69). In keeping with the investigative thrust in the book, I add on to Bartholomew's observation that v. 11b also affirms the mystery of God, which is beyond human comprehension—'yet no one can fathom what God has done from beginning to end' (v. 11b). The final obscure phrase in v. 15 (literally it can be rendered: 'But God seeks out what has been pursued', v. 15b) appears disjunctive with the first half of the verse. It has generated a host of diverse scholarly opinions. Seow suggests that 'God seeks all matters which are beyond human grasp' (Seow 1997: 174). In connecting 1.9 and 3.15a together, Crenshaw's interpretation of v. 15b has received general agreement. Verse 15b replies to why there is nothing new under the sun—'Because God ensures that events which have just transpired do not vanish into thin air. God brings them back once more, so that the past circles into the future' (Crenshaw 1987: 100; cf. Enns 2011: 56; Fox 1999: 213-14).

Unpacking the above overall framework, reading the passage as poetry, v. 1 presents the first parallel pair. 'Time' in the first line parallels 'season' (though using a different Hebrew word) in the second line. The second line extends the idea of 'everything' with the extension 'every activity under the heavens' as an alternative articulation of 'under the sun'. The next fourteen pairs of contrasting concepts in vv. 2-8 highlight the function of the second-person wisdom's voice. It evokes the need of discernment for humanity to know the right course of action at any given time (also Heim 2019: 69). The momentum of development in the list moves from human activities (applicable to both large scale and individualistic) to human emotions in vv. 4, 8a ('a time to weep and a time to laugh'; 'a time to mourn and a time to dance'; 'a time to love and a time to hate'). As to the precise meanings and relationships within the pairs behind the metaphorical presentations (e.g. 'to kill and 'to heal', v. 3; 'to keep and to throw away', v. 6b), I concur with Heim that readers should not seek for only one correct interpretation (2019: 70). In terms of appropriation, it is widely open to all readerly responses, as I believe it is the original intent of the collective voice of wisdom here.

Readers can appreciate the dialogic dynamics in reading Ecclesiastes polyphonically here. Verse 9 marks the merger of the second-person collective voice of wisdom and Qohelet's 'I'-voice. Qohelet poses another rhetorical question ('What do workers gain from their toil'; cf. 1.3). The first audience should be able to answer with an absolute 'Nothing!' (Longman 1998: 118). In his 'I'-voice, Qohelet provides the answer. He states that he 'has seen' (firsthand personal experience) the burden God has laid on humanity (v. 10). Also, God has 'put all times (past and present) in the human heart' (v. 11a, in the sense that God gives humanity 'the demanding challenge of understanding the significance of their lives and activity [Goldingay 2021a:132]'). Qohelet then presents three affirmations. *First,* God is sovereign, and he preordains everything fitting in its time (v. 11a). Yet, it is all mystery to the human mind as to what God has done from beginning to end (v. 11c parallels v. 11b). *Second,* in his personal experience (the Hebrew word 'know', referring to one's experiential knowledge), he affirms the opportunity to be happy (v. 12), and the ability to eat, drink and find satisfaction in toil is the gift from God. *Third,* in another confessional statement through his firsthand experience (I 'know'), he affirms God's sovereignty in his order of ruling in human lives (v. 14a). The purpose behind Qohelet's firsthand observations leading to this affirmation is: 'So that people will fear him' (14b). This is perhaps the overall encompassing message of this unit.

2. Second *carpe diem* saying (3.12-13) and the ending (3.14-15)

¹² I know that there is nothing better for people than to be happy and to do good while they live. ¹³ That each of them may eat and drink and find satisfaction in all their toil—this is the gift of God. ¹⁴ I know that everything God does will endure forever; nothing can be added to it, and nothing taken from it. God does it so that people will fear him.

¹⁵ Whatever is has already been,
 and what will be has been before;
 and God will call the past to account.

Verses 12-13 have been perceived as the second *carpe diem* saying in Ecclesiastes. It is presented in the context of the answer to the rhetorical question in 3.9 (precisely, there is 'no' profit for workers from their toil). Again, it is within one of Qohelet's confessional responses. Even the opportunity for enjoyment and being happy is a gift from the sovereign God. Lee has pointed out that 'to do good while they live' in v. 12 has moral connotations in the Hebrew Bible (see Gen. 26.29; Deut. 6.18; Judg. 9.16). By juxtaposing the expression 'to do good' with the explicit call 'to enjoy', 'Qohelet intimates that the enjoyment of life is indeed a matter of ethical duty' (Lee

2015: 41). Thus 'enjoyment is always contingent upon God's giving and is an opportunity available only for the *moment*' (41, *italics* mine).

The closing verse (v. 15a) *reinforces* the poem in 1.9-11. There is nothing new under the sun as God is in control of all time and seasons in human life. Humanity can have nothing to do about it. The last phrase in this verse ignites much discussion. It appears incoherent with v. 15a, and the literal translation goes: 'And God seeks out what has been pursued'. Linking this with the idea of the mystery of God, it could be understood as 'God seeks out those matters that are beyond human grasp' (Seow 1997: 174). Alternatively, Fox opts for the idea that God ensures that the past events would not just vanish, and God will bring back once more, so that the past circles into the present (Fox 1999: 213-14). If Qohelet's challenge in vv. 12-14 is for humanity to do good (moral connotation), be happy and to enjoy life (God's gift) as we can, and if v. 15b is understood the way as presented above, I suggest here v. 15b to be read as 'God will ensure that all human pursuits be accomplished in the way he sees fit'. The ambiguity created in this verse opens another opportunity for readers to make their own interpretive choice.

E. Qohelet's First-Person Voice Reflecting on his 'Exploration of Life' in Dialogue with his Inner Voice (3.16–4.16)

1. First cycle of exploration (3.16-21)

[16] And I saw something else under the sun:

In the place of judgment—wickedness was there,
  in the place of justice—wickedness was there.

[17] I said to myself,

'God will bring into judgment
  both the righteous and the wicked,
for there will be a time for every activity,
  a time to judge every deed'.

[18] I also said to myself, 'As for humans, God tests them so that they may see that they are like the animals. [19] Surely the fate of human beings is like that of the animals; the same fate awaits them both: As one dies, so dies the other. All have the same breath; humans have no advantage over animals. Everything is meaningless. [20] All go to the same place; all come from dust, and to dust all return. [21] Who knows if the human spirit rises upward and if the spirit of the animal goes down into the earth?'

Many commentators see 3.1-15 as concluding the first section of Ecclesiastes. One transition is clear. Qohelet's reflections in 1.3–3.15 are arising from his *personal* life experience under the sun. Reading Ecclesiastes from the perspective of a memoir, Qohelet shares with his audience what he has accomplished, his achievements during the prime of his life. He flourished in all aspects that we would expect for a man. Starting from 3.16 (until 10.7), he changes the focus to his *intentional* exploration in life. His explorations and observations extend to different spheres of humanity's collective lived experience under the sun—that is, the Grand Narrative, regardless of whether you are a person of royalty or a commoner among the audience. The slices of the reality are to be understood as universal truths. These are deep reflections, indicating the escalating and deepening momentum in building up the cumulative repertoire of Qohelet's reflective wisdom through his explorations in life.

The particular phrase 'I saw/have seen' (v. 16) is characteristic in this first cycle of exploration. Again, 'saying to his own heart' provides a platform for his reflections (vv. 17-18). Reading the book dialogically, his inner self joins in the vibrant dialogue with Qohelet's 'I'-voice. Qohelet begins the exploration with the opening 'and again I saw under the sun' (v. 16). He witnessed 'in the place of justice, there is wickedness; and in the place of righteousness, there is wickedness'. As a parallel pair, justice and righteousness are often used interchangeably. He then turns inward with his observation and dialogues with his own heart—'I said in my heart'—and utters a confessional statement: 'God will bring into judgment both the righteous and the wicked'. God will bring both to judgment at the appointed time (v. 17). Qohelet's reflection goes inward as he converses with his inner self again, pondering the issue of death. As one of the major themes in Ecclesiastes, the matter appears here again (see 3.2a). As Chloe Sun observed, the attitude of Ecclesiastes on death is quite distinct (Sun 2017: 206). Verses 18-20 precisely state that God uses death to test humanity; humans have the same fate as animals: death awaits them both. They all go to the same place; all come from dust and to dust they return (v. 20). This inward reflection ends with another outcry, echoing the motto: 'All is vanity!' (v. 19b). It is then followed by a rhetorical question, 'Who knows?'—'If the human spirit rises upward and if the spirit of the animal goes down into the earth' (v. 21)? Apparently, v. 21 creates another obscurity. This underscores the notion of dialectic in the book, which surfaces sporadically throughout the twelve chapters. A reading that embraces dialectic textual tensions will better enhance the meaning-significance of Ecclesiastes. Focusing on the flow of Qohelet's emotive response at this junction, he utters the third *carpe diem saying* in v. 22.

2. Third *carpe diem* saying (3.22)

²² So I saw that there is nothing better for humans than to enjoy their works, because that is their lot. For who can bring them to see what will happen after them?[8]

A threefold observation is to be noted in this *carpe diem* saying. *First,* the reason for rejoicing here is humanity's 'works' ('So I saw that there is nothing better for humans than to enjoy their works' vs. 'burden' and 'toil' in 2.18-21; 3.9.) *Second,* the new element added here is the reference to 'portion' (or 'lot', as a plot of land acquired as a grant; see Ps. 16.5-6). Lee further comments that 'it is hardly surprising that Qohelet would speak of toil and the possibility of joy in one breath' (Lee 2005: 43; cf. 2.10, 24; 3.13; 5.18 [MT 17]; 8.15). Enjoying one's work is far better than anything else. Further, the 'works'/ability to work is God's gift, our 'lot'. *Third,* the verse ends with another rhetorical question: 'For who can bring them to see what will happen after them?' The temporal, immediate response to enjoyment is meant here. God's gift is referred to as our 'lot/portion'. The notion of human responsibility to *cultivate* our lot or to *manage* our portion is to be perceived as part of humanity's enjoyment of work.

3. *Second cycle of exploration (4.1-3)*

4

¹ Again I returned[9] and saw all the oppression that was taking place under the sun:
   I saw the tears of the oppressed—
     and they have no comforter;
   power was on the side of their oppressors—
     and they have no comforter.
² And I declared that the dead,
    who had already died,
   are happier than the living,
    who are still alive.
³ But better than both
   is the one who has never been born,
   who has not seen the evil
    that is done under the sun.

---

8. For gender-inclusive purposes, singular 'the man' is changed to plural: 'humans'; therefore, their/them, and 'works' in plural.

9. Literally, 'I returned', in the sense of 'Again I turned and saw', beginning another cycle of exploration in life, also v. 7.

Starting from this second cycle of exploration up to the seventeenth in 10.5-7, Qohelet uses a characteristic phrase 'So I turned and saw' (v. 1). The Hebrew word for 'turn' (*šûb*) signifies a 180-degree turning, also used to refer to repentance in the Hebrew Bible (e.g. Isa. 30.15; 49.5). In this context of Qohelet's exploration in life, it points to an intentional, active initiation to explore different facets of humanity's life under the sun ('Again I turned and saw'). This 'turning' leads to seeing the tears of the oppressed who have no comforter and realizing that power was on the side of their oppressors (v. 1). Qohelet's active action ('turning') leads to his 'seeing', and 'seeing' is advancing to 'perceiving' (i.e. 'the power is always on the side of the oppressor', v. 1b). He then comes to the reflective summary appraisal: The dead are happier than the living (v. 2)! After this bold declaration, he utters a deeply emotive conclusion—'But better than both is the one who has never been born, who has not seen the evil that is done under the sun' (v. 4). This escalating summary (from exploring [v. 1a] → perceiving [v. 1b] → declaration [v. 2] → lament [v. 3]) is weighty and bitter, for it denies what he sets off to do in the explorations (2.9-15, 17). Starting from here, the cycle of 'turning/seeing → perceiving → concluding' stands out in the explorations that follow (See Leung Lai 2014: 214-17).

4. Third cycle of exploration (4.4)

Interlude: Second-person wisdom sayings (4.5-6)

⁴ And I saw that all toil and all achievement spring from one person's envy of another. This too is vanity, a chasing after the wind.
⁵ *Fools fold their hands*
 and ruin themselves.
⁶ *Better one handful with tranquillity*
 than two handfuls with toil
 and chasing after the wind.

The same momentum of exploration is witnessed in this one verse. 'Then I saw ...' (v. 4a) and perceived that 'all toil and all achievement spring from one person's envy of another' (v. 4b). Qohelet then concludes with the heavy outcry—'All is vanity, a chasing after the wind', echoing the same emotive response in the previous three chapters.

In the **Interlude**, the second-person wisdom's voice joins in—'Fools fold their hands and ruin themselves. Better one handful with tranquillity than two handfuls with toil and chasing after the wind' (vv. 5-6). Using the characteristic 'better than' saying in the book, this second-person wisdom saying carries a positive notion and begins the narration about fools/foolishness versus wise/wisdom in the following chapters. In keeping with the wisdom literature of the Old Testament, this subject matter of 'fools and wise' also illustrates the polar structure of Ecclesiastes.

5. Fourth cycle of exploration (4.7-16)

Interlude: Second-person wisdom sayings (4.9-14)
Reflective summary: 'This too is vanity, a chasing after the wind!'
(4.15-16)

⁷ Again I returned and saw something meaningless under the sun:
⁸ There was a man all alone;
   he had neither son nor brother.
There was no end to his toil,
   yet his eyes were not content with his wealth.
'For whom am I toiling', he asked,
   'and why am I depriving myself of enjoyment?'[10]
This too is vanity—
   and an evil task!

Verse 7 begins with the familiar formula: 'Again I turned and saw vanity under the sun'. The sphere of Qohelet's exploration now turns to a miserable case in humanity's family life: a man who is alone and toils diligently all his lifetime. However, though he is still not content with his wealth, he has neither a son nor a brother to inherit his wealth (v. 8a). For the first time in the book, we find that Qohelet in his 'I'-narration cites another interior monologue in the case of a lonely man. The man asked his inner self, 'For whom am I toiling, and why am I depriving myself of enjoyment (literally, 'my soul from good' v. 8b)? This interior monologue within Qohelet's 'I'-discourse carries an additional deep reflective flavor. Building on the sentiment expressed in this rhetorical question uttered by the lonely man, Qohelet breaks out in distress: 'This too is vanity—and an evil task' (v. 8)! In this case study, we see the same cycle of Qohelet's reflective, self-engaged exploration. It proceeds from turning → seeing → perceiving/reflecting through an interior monologue → concluding statement.

Interlude: Second-person wisdom sayings (4.9-14)

⁹ *Two are better than one,*
   because they have a good return for their labor:

---

10. Literally, 'depriving my soul from good'.

> *¹⁰ If either of them falls down,
>   one can help the other up.
> But pity anyone who falls
>   and has no one to help them up.*
> *¹¹ Also, if two lie down together, they will keep warm.
>   But how can one keep warm alone?*
> *¹² Two can defend themselves.
> A cord of three strands is not quickly broken.*

¹³ Better a poor but wise youth than an old but foolish king who no longer knows how to heed a warning. ¹⁴ The youth may have come from prison to the kingship, or he may have been born in poverty within his kingdom.

The second-person wisdom's voice joins in after Qohelet's negative concluding statement (vv. 9-14), providing positive advice on the subject: 'what is the good/the better?' Readers witness a case where a three-way dialogue is in place: (1) Qohelet's 'I'-reflective voice (vv. 7-8); (2) the 'interior monologic' voice of the lonely man (v. 8b); and (3) the voice of wisdom (vv. 9-14). The interaction among the three enhances the elucidation of the truth on 'what is the good/the better'. This truth is brought about through Qohelet's eye-witnessed observation, the lived experience of a lonely man and the collective voice of wisdom, Qohelet's pretext (i.e. rooted in centuries of cumulative wisdom of the ancient society of Israel).

Following the theme of 'loneliness' in Qohelet's exploration in vv. 7-8, using a 'better than' saying, wisdom's voice affirms in vv. 13-14 the advantage of being in the company of others. Wisdom cites four practical examples along the idea 'two are better than one': (1) in coworking (v. 9); (2) in providing mutual support (v. 10); (3) in keeping warm (v. 11); and (4) in protection (v. 12a). She sums up with an analysis: 'A cord of three strands is not quickly broken' (v. 12b), and using another 'better than' example, wisdom's voice employs another analogy—'better is a poor but wise youth than an old but foolish king who no longer knows how to heed a warning' (v. 13). Wisdom further presents three contrasting concepts to highlight the value of wisdom in opposition to foolishness: (1) a wise youth versus a foolish king; (2) in captivity contrasted with kingship; and (3) living in poverty in opposition to living in the abundance of the kingdom.

Reflective Summary: 'This too is vanity, a chasing after the wind'
         (vv. 15-16)

¹⁵ I saw that all who lived and walked under the sun followed the youth, the king's successor. ¹⁶ There was no end to all the people who were before them. But those who came later were not pleased with the successor. Surely[11] this too is vanity, a chasing after the wind.[12]

Following wisdom's voice on the comparison between a wise youth and a foolish king (vv. 13-14), Qohelet perceived ('I saw') that all those who lived and walked under the sun followed the youth (literally, 'the second child who shall stand up in his place'), the king's successor (v. 15). It points to the popularity of the underprivileged youth who rose to power in place of a foolish king. Verse 16 is ambiguous, and it is open to different translations. An irony surfaces if v. 16 is understood as Qohelet's witness to the popularity of the wise youth rising from his status to be the king's successor. Yet, a setback happened; those people who came afterwards were not pleased with the king's successor, the wise youth. In response to this reverse outcome (from popularity to displeasure), Qohelet utters a distressing summary appraisal in this cycle of exploration: 'All is vanity, a chasing after the wind' (v. 16)! The impact of this observation is explicated behind the 'I saw'. It is more than an isolated case study, but one that is witnessed by Qohelet through his engaged observations of human lived experience under the sun. Reading Ecclesiastes dialectically and in a 'cross-graining' fashion (in this case, the reversal is from 'popularity' [i.e. one grain-running directionality] to 'displeasure' [another grain-running directionality]), one should allow the dialectics or contradictions to stand side by side as coexisting realities. Readers are not expected to resolve all these polar tensions, but to tune in to the mode of 'sustaining in tension'. I see this as an important message of the book. In fact, sustaining in polar tensions is the most dynamic elucidation of the hows of humanity's 'living under the sun'.

F. Second-Person Wisdom's Instruction on 'Fearing God' (5.1-7 [MT 4.17-5.6])

Interlude: Wisdom sayings (5.8-12 [MT 5.7-11])

5[13]

¹ Guard your steps when you go to the house of God. Go near to listen rather than to offer the sacrifice of fools, who do not know that they do wrong.

---

11. Untranslated in NIV.
12. The ambiguity of vv. 14-16 makes all translations and hence interpretations uncertain. NIV's translation here makes good sense to readers (see Murphy 1992: 40-43).
13. 5.1-20 (MT = Hebrew Bible 4.17–5.19)

² *Do not be quick with your mouth,*
   do not be hasty in your heart
   to utter anything before God.
  God is in heaven
   and you are on earth,
   so let your words be few.
³ *A dream comes when there are many cares,*
   and many words mark the speech of a fool.
⁴ *When you make a vow to God, do not delay to fulfill it. God has no pleasure in fools; fulfill your vow.* ⁵ *It is better not to make a vow than to make one and not fulfill it.* ⁶ *Do not let your mouth lead you into sin. And do not protest to the temple messenger, 'My vow was a mistake'. Why should God be angry at what you say and destroy the work of your hands?* ⁷ *Much dreaming and many words are vanities. Therefore, fear God.*

With respect to the flow of thought between the previous section and the second-person wisdom's instruction here, Peter Enns points out that at the end of Qohelet's discursive narration on the perils of royal succession, he moves to another sovereign, God himself (Enns 2011: 65). Seow also notes that 5.1-7 [MT 4.17–5.6]) moves from the body of reflective language to that of wisdom's instructions (Seow 1997: 197). This passage is full of 'imperatives' (e.g. 'Guard your steps', v. 1 [MT 4.17]; 'do not be quick', 'do not be hasty', v. 2 [MT 1]; 'Therefore fear God', v. 7 [MT 6]). The second-person wisdom's voice here is authoritative. After cautioning the audience regarding the manner in which one should approach God (v. 1 [MT 4.17]), wisdom's voice adds five warnings: (1) 'do not be quick with your mouth' (v. 2 [MT 1], with v. 3b [MT 2b] alluding to the wordy speech of a fool, which is parallel to the many dreams one makes and are deemed meaningless/vanities, v. 7 [MT 6]); (2) 'do not be hasty in your heart' (v. 2 [MT 1]); (3) 'do not be wordy' (vv. 2-3 [MT 1-2]); (4) 'do not delay in fulfilling vows made to God (vv. 5, 6b [MT 4, 5b]); and (5) 'do not let your mouth lead you to sin' (v. 6 [MT 5]). The overall depiction here is that God is to be feared; therefore, be cautious with proper manner when you approach God.

The passage ends with the second-person wisdom's final instruction: 'Therefore fear God'. Enns sees that the 'fearing God' here is not the *same* fear as in Prov. 1.7, 'The fear of the Lord is the beginning of wisdom'. 'God is in heaven, and you are on earth' speaks to the remoteness between God and humans. This distance creates the 'fear' in humans toward God, 'whose inscrutable acts produce pain, anxiety, frustration—fear' (Enns 2011: 69; contra Bartholomew 2009: 208-209). My interpretation differs from Enns's on three grounds: *First,* the passage is wisdom's instructions, Qohelet's pretext. It is hardly the case that we can take the concept as distinct from the motto of the book of Proverbs on 'fear of the Lord' and 'wisdom' (cf. Prov. 1.7). *Second,* vv. 1-7 [MT 4.17–5.6] are wisdom's instructions on the proper attitude of worship, that is, when humans approach God. The first audience is encouraged to follow wisdom's instructions out of the fear of God. Likewise, Goldingay (2021a: 172) also sees vv. 1-8 [MT 4.17–5.7]) as a positive exhortation to be 'in awe of God'. 'Fear', then, is an attitude for worshippers, not a product generated by observing the acts of God in human affairs (e.g. 3.13-14), along with pain, anxiety and bewilderment. *Third,* up to ch. 5, we observe the pattern of positive affirmations amid the pessimistic notions (cf. 2.3, 13, 24-26; 3.12-14, in context). 'Therefore, fear God' carries the same positive and exhortative vigour as the ending of wisdom's voice in 3.14-15.

Interlude: Wisdom sayings (5.8-12 [MT 5.7-11])

⁸ If you see the poor oppressed in a district, and justice and rights denied, do not be surprised at such things; for one official is eyed by a higher one, and over them both are others higher still. ⁹ The increase from the land is taken by all; the king himself profits from the fields.

¹⁰ Whoever loves money never has enough;
 whoever loves wealth is never satisfied with their income.
 This too is vanity.
¹¹ As goods increase,
 so do those who consume them.
 And what benefit are they to the owners
 except to feast their eyes on them?
¹² The sleep of a laborer is sweet,
 whether they eat little or much,
 but as for the rich, their abundance
 permits them no sleep.

In the **Interlude** of wisdom's voice in vv. 8-12 (MT 7-11), the language changes from 'imperative instructions' to that of 'sayings'. Following the train of thought about justice and righteousness (v. 8 [MT 7]), wisdom continues her voice. Portraying a picture of the normality of cases of injustice among high officials (v. 8 [MT 7]), wisdom's critique of the king in gaining profits from the people creates another negative notion (v. 9 [MT 8]; cf. the comparison of the foolish king and the wise youth in 4.13-14). Along the same line, Krüger also notes that v. 8 could be read as a radical critique of government organization. The 'king' could be referred to as a 'culmination' of a system in which each 'more highly placed one' strives solely for his own advantage' (2004: 115). Heim points out the progression from intentional ambiguity in v. 8 (MT 7) to calculated hyper-ambiguity in v. 9 (MT 8) as in v. 9 [MT 8], the monarch is mentioned in a statement that can also be read both as a defense and as a radical critique. Taking the book as a written record of a speech sequence like the routines of modern stand-up comedians (who use the medium of comedy to critique problematic issues), Heim demonstrates that v. 8 (MT 7) is a classic case illustrating the function of underdeterminate language. It creates plausible deniability in case the book's regime-critical potential were discovered by those it meant to critique (cf. Heim 2019: 96-97; Jarick 2014: 176-88).

By means of parallelism, wisdom is contrasting the discontent and unhappiness of the wealthy, who love 'silver/money' (i.e. their wealth does not allow them to sleep), to the 'satisfaction/enjoyment' of life's basic needs (i.e. 'good sleep' and 'sweet dreams') of the laborers, who toil under the sun (vv. 10-12 [MT 9-11]).

G. Qohelet's First-Person Exploration of Life Continued (5.13–6.12 [MT 5.12-6.12])

1. Fifth cycle of exploration (5.13-17 [MT 5.12-16])

¹³ I have seen a grievous evil under the sun:
  Wealth hoarded to the harm of its owners,
¹⁴ or wealth lost through some misfortune,
 so that when they¹⁴ have children
  there is nothing left for them to inherit.
¹⁵ Everyone comes naked from their mother's womb,
  and as everyone comes, so they depart.
 They take nothing from their toil
  that they can carry in their hands.

¹⁶ This too is a grievous evil:

As everyone comes, so they depart,
  and what do they gain,
   since they toil for the wind?
¹⁷ All their days they eat in darkness,
  with great frustration, affliction and anger.

---

14. The personal pronouns in vv. 13-17 [MT 12-16] are all in the third-person singular. For gender-inclusive purpose, the translations here are in the third-person plural.

Consistent with Qohelet's cycles of exploration, the passage begins with 'There is a grievous evil I have seen under the sun' (5.13 [MT 12]). Verses 13-17 [MT 12-16] represent the most distressing reflection of Qohelet's explorations. Stuart Weeks translated v. 13 [MT 12] as 'There is something painfully bad I have seen underneath the sun' (Weeks 2021: 1). Heim takes Qohelet's exploration here as an 'emotionally catastrophic event, a particularly sickening misfortune' (Heim 2019: 99). Qohelet's narration from here to ch. 7 provides profound insights on wealth, satisfaction and misery.

The scenario laid out here is about an instance of wealth hoarded by its owner and lost through some misfortunate deeds, leading to the owner's own misery. It is described as when the owner later fathers a son, he has left nothing for the child to inherit (vv. 13-14 [MT 12-13]). Whether Qohelet cited a generic case yet realistic enough to be representative of a wide range of human experience (Heim 2019: 100), or a particular eye-witnessed event is not the point here (contra Weeks's metaphorical interpretation, 2021: 2). The significance lies in the fact that Qohelet perceives the scenario elucidated here as something that is painfully distressing: overstocking material goods for one's own sake is futile. He then presents his reflective appraisal in v. 16a [MT 15a]: 'This too is a grievous evil!' Going back to the view of death in Ecclesiastes, in the form of a summary, he utters, 'as he came, shall he depart', followed by a rhetorical question: 'what profit (is it) for him who has toiled for the wind?' He ends with extremely harsh words—'All his days, he eats in darkness, with great sorrow/frustration, affliction and anger' (v. 16 [MT 15]).

The emotive words expressed above are quite weighty. Reading Ecclesiastes as Qohelet's *memoir,* and *narratively,* here the first audience witnessed an older man, Qohelet, narrating out of his self-engaged life explorations (he has seen it with his own eyes: 'There is a grievous evil I have seen under the sun', v. 13 [MT 12]). He attested to the miserable outcome of one's 'hoarding of wealth', which is devastating. On the one hand, the decedent will leave with no inheritance. On the other hand, one will spend the rest of one's life in true misery, sorrow/frustration, affliction and anger. Reading Ecclesiastes *narratively,* as Qohelet identifies himself with his community's 'hoarding wealth', flesh-and-blood lived experience here, he finds himself overwhelmed with these sickening emotions. Yet to his readers, a *memoir* reading provides a platform, a vehicle for Qohelet to pour out without restraint his feelings and felt emotions. In this sense, this is not so much a memoir *of* Qohelet; it is a memoir written by Qohelet and *for* himself. He needs this vehicle to carry his deep emotions and feelings.

2. Fourth *carpe diem* saying (5.18-20 [MT 5.17-19])

[18] Behold![15] This is what I have observed to be good: that it is appropriate for a person to eat, to drink and to find satisfaction in their toilsome labor under the sun during the few days of life God has given them—for this is their lot. [19] Moreover, when God gives someone wealth and possessions, and the ability to enjoy them, to accept their lot and be happy in their toil—this is a gift of God. [20] They seldom reflect on the days of their life, because God keeps them occupied with gladness of heart.

Qohelet's 'I'-narration takes a sudden twist in vv. 18-20 [MT 17-19]), from an extremely distressed mood to that of exhilarating exhortations. With an idiomatic opening, 'Behold, this is what I have observed to be good' (v. 18 [MT 17] vs. v. 13 [MT 12]: 'This is a grievous evil ...'), Qohelet begins the fourth *carpe diem* saying. Capturing the attention of the audience, Qohelet utters, 'behold! come and see', there is indeed something 'good' under the sun—'it is appropriate for people to eat and drink, and to experience good in the fruit of all their toil.' (cf. 3.11, 13). William Brown names eating, drinking, and enjoying one's work as the 'three gifts of joy/a trinity of delight' (Brown 2000: 62). Verse 19 [MT 18] forms a sharp contrast to v. 17 [MT 16]. This *carpe diem* saying is distinct from the previous ones on three grounds. *First,* it is the first time that enjoying one's labor is considered as God's gift; it is their 'lot' (v. 18b [MT 17b]). *Second,* earthly wealth and possession are God's gifts also (v. 19 [MT 18]). Verse 19 [MT 18] goes deeper on the threefold dimension of God's gift: 'the ability to enjoy', 'acceptance of God's allotment' and 'be happy in one's labor'. *Third,* two notions are underscored here: (1) the 'lot' given by God includes wealth and possessions; and (2) the God-given 'lot' is repeated twice (v. 18b [MT 17b], and 'this is a gift of God', v. 19 [MT 18]). In its immediate context, 'lot' (or portion), on the one hand, points to the gift of God. On the other hand, it includes the idea of God-given possessions and wealth. 'Lot' in the rest of the Old Testament often refers to the inheritance from God in the form of a piece of land (e.g. Gen. 31.14; Lev. 6.1; Ps. 16.5). Against this background, other than being human's responsibility to enjoy the gift from God, 'lot' further implies it is humanity's duty to cultivate this piece of land and to manage well the God-given possessions and wealth.

Verse 20 [MT 19] highlights further the antithetical nature of the exhortation here as compared to the previous section (vv. 13-17 [MT 12-16]). It presents a startling contrast in that the one who hoards wealth will eat in darkness, with great sorrow, affliction and anger (v. 17 [MT 16]). Yet as for

---

15. Untranslated in NIV.

the one who is granted God's gift, God will keep him occupied with gladness in his heart (v. 19 [MT 18]).

3. Sixth cycle of exploration (6.1-12)

6

¹ I have seen another evil under the sun, and it weighs heavily on humanity:
² God gives some people wealth, possessions, and honor, so that they lack nothing their hearts desire, but God does not grant them the ability to enjoy them, and strangers enjoy them instead. This is vanity, a grievous evil.

³ A person may have a hundred children and live many years; yet no matter how long he lives, if he cannot enjoy his prosperity and does not receive proper burial, I say that a stillborn child is better off than he. ⁴ It comes without meaning, it departs in darkness, and in darkness its name is shrouded. ⁵ Though it never saw the sun or knew anything, it has more rest than does that man— ⁶ even if he lives a thousand years twice over but fails to enjoy his prosperity. Do not all go to the same place?

⁷ Everyone's toil is for their mouth,
   yet their appetite is never satisfied.
⁸ What advantage have the wise over fools?
  What do the poor gain
   by knowing how to conduct themselves before others?
⁹ Better what the eye sees
   than the roving of the appetite.
  This too is vanity,
   a chasing after the wind.
¹⁰ Whatever exists has already been named,
   and what humanity is has been known;
  no one can contend
   with someone who is stronger.
¹¹ The more the words,
   the less the meaning,
   and how does that profit anyone?

¹² For who knows what is good for a person in life, during the few and meaningless days they pass through like a shadow? Who can tell them what will happen under the sun after they are gone?

In between the observation of two cases of grievous evil (5.15-17 [MT 14-16] and 6.1-12) is an uplifting *carpe diem* saying (5.18-20 [MT 17-19]). This provides a heartening message to the first audience amidst the dreadful situation as described in 6.1-12. Qohelet's sixth cycle of exploration begins with the same diction as the previous one in 5.13-17 (MT 5.12-16): 'I have seen/witnessed another evil under the sun'. Further, this evil 'weighs heavily on humanity' (v. 1). Heim notes that the flow of thought in 6.1-12 moves from the common cause of misery in vv. 1-2 to a specific cause of misery despite abundant wealth, property and prestige (vv. 3-9), and ends with a reflection on the idea that the pursuit of happiness through material affluence is a mirage, as demonstrated in 5.13–6.9 (2019: 119-20). Other than this 'from common to specific' chain of thought, vv. 3-9a develop into a heightening description, building up to the escalating effect of another anguished cry in v. 9b: 'This too is vanity, a chasing after the wind!'

Philip Ryken takes 6.1-12 as 'one of the Bible's darkest chapters' (2010: 140). Qohelet points to the common human misery in that God grants people all the goodness of life that the human heart would desire. However, God does not grant them the ability to enjoy it, but strangers enjoy it instead (v. 2). He then responds with the same agonizing cry: 'This is vanity, a grievous evil' (v. 2b)! After vv. 1-2a, the direness of the situation is further elaborated in vv. 2b-9, and the focus moves from wealth and possession to the longevity of life. Using a series of six rhetorical questions in vv. 6, 8 (2x), 11 and 12 (2x), Qohelet powerfully brings the dreadfulness of human misery to the forefront of his observations, with lingering effect. Rhetorical questions here function to provoke the first audience to think deeply along the various aspects of the probing question 'what is good?' Goldingay notes that there are three contrasting forms of rhetoric describing the dire situation (see 2021a: 187-89), and Qohelet invites the readerly imagination here. *First,* to the Hebrew mind, it is tragic if strangers (those outside of the family) get to enjoy the inheritance of people's property and wealth instead. *Second*, if a man lives many years and fathers many children, if he cannot enjoy his property and receive no proper burial (esp. proper burial is considered as a blessed life, a blessing from God; see Gen. 35.19-20, 28-29; Josh. 24.29-30), then the abundance of descendants and the longevity of life will be greatly damaged. *Third,* using the analysis of a 'stillborn child' who comes and departs in darkness and with no burial and no name to be remembered, the stillborn is even better than the one who lives a long life but fails to enjoy all his prosperity (vv. 3-6). The rhetorical question in v. 6b—'Do not all go to the same place?'—introduces a more intense probe through the lingering effect among the first audience. They all end up in darkness with no burial!

Many have noted the issue of incoherence in vv. 7-12 (see Goldingay 2021a: 188-89; Enns 2011: 76-77). Following the thought development, I seek to make some sense out of this difficult passage with the following statements: (1) Humans toil to feed themselves, but their efforts cannot satisfy their desires (v. 7). (2) The wise may not have advantage over the fools (v. 8a). (3) The poor may not have any gain even if they know how to conduct themselves before others (v. 8b). (4) Better is what the eye sees than the roving of the appetite (v. 9a). (I have adopted Enns's proposed meaning here: 'The sight of the eyes' is better than 'the passing of life', 2011: 76.) Simply put, 'life is better than death'. On the surface, these four are the random thoughts of Qohelet. However, cast against the context of the two rhetorical questions in v. 8, Qohelet is simply encouraging his first audience to reflect with their emotive response on the outcome of his observation: There is no advantage for the wise, or the fools who manage their life well, since they can never find satisfaction through their labor. Yet, life is still better than death (v. 9a, following the chain of thought of the stillborn child in v. 3-6). He concludes with the same agonizing cry: 'This too is vanity, a chasing after the wind' (v. 9b)!

In vv. 10-12, Qohelet expresses his frustration in the form of three lamenting rhetorical questions (vv. 11, 12a and 12b). As Enns notes, the essence of 6.9-12 is basically, 'nothing changes, and you cannot do anything about it' (2011: 77). The word 'contends' (v. 10) in Hebrew means 'judge' and is used mostly with God as the subject (e.g. Jer. 5.28; Ps. 135.14). When used with humans as the subject, it carries the idea of 'defend, argue, plea' (e.g. Jer. 30.13; 2 Sam. 19.9). 'No one can contend with someone who is stronger (God)' (v. 10b). For one will find all arguing words with God are nothing but 'vanity' and offer no profit (v. 11). Qohelet concludes his sixth cycle of exploration in life with a depressing notion. Followed by the rhetorical questions posed in v. 11b, 'who knows', and 'who can tell' in v. 12, the depiction here touches the core of his frustration. Humans simply do not know what is good in life during the meaningless days they pass through life like a shadow. There is nothing concrete that they can grasp or remember. They cannot plan for or anticipate the future before they die (v. 12).

While Enns boldly remarks that the theme surfaced here is 'life is absurd, you die anyway, and God is to blame', I see it quite differently. Journeying through the sixth cycle of his life exploration with the intentionality of 'turning and seeing', Qohelet shares honestly with his audience the outcome of his deep reflections. He arrives at the point of finding himself facing the need of downloading all his frustration, laments, humanness before the God who is stronger than him and abides in heaven. This is again his affirmation, despite the emotive upheaval, and he intentionally hides the identity of 'the one who is stronger'. Apparently, there is no intimacy in the God–Qohelet relationship. There is always a distance between God who is in heavens and Qohelet who abides on earth. His inquiring and investigative spirit is hindered by the dire situation he has witnessed in his community. Reading 6.1-12 as an episode of his memoir, Qohelet uses the literary medium of six rhetorical questions (vv. 6, 8 [2x], 11, 12 [2x]) as a double-edged sword, to dialogue with his audience and to provoke them to reflect on the absurdity of life.

As one of the darkest chapters in the Bible, 6.1-12 is revealing slices of the reality in the flesh-and-blood lived experience of humanity under the sun.

H. Second-Person Wisdom Sayings (7.1-14)

1. 'Better than' sayings (7.1-12)

7

¹ *A good name is better than fine perfume,*
  and the day of death better than the day of birth.
² *It is better to go to a house of mourning*
  than to go to a house of feasting,
 for death is the destiny of everyone;
  the living should take this to heart.
³ *Frustration is better than laughter,*
  because a sad face is good for the heart.
⁴ *The heart of the wise is in the house of mourning,*
  but the heart of fools is in the house of pleasure.
⁵ *It is better to heed the rebuke of a wise person*
  than to listen to the song of fools.
⁶ *Like the crackling of thorns under the pot,*
  so is the laughter of fools.
  This too is vanity!
⁷ *Extortion turns a wise person into a fool,*
  and a bribe corrupts the heart.
⁸ *The end of a matter is better than its beginning,*
  and patience is better than pride.
⁹ *Do not be quickly provoked in your spirit,*
  for anger resides in the lap of fools.
¹⁰ *Do not say, 'Why were the old days better than these?'*
  For it is not wise to ask such questions.
¹¹ *Wisdom, like an inheritance, is a good thing*
  and benefits those who see the sun.
¹² *Wisdom is a shelter*
  as money is a shelter,
 but the advantage of knowledge is this:
  Wisdom preserves those who have it.

The collective voice of wisdom begins to speak after Qohelet's depressive depiction of the dire situation of human experience under the sun in ch. 6. In a way, wisdom's voice carries on the subject matter discussed in ch. 6 (on 'what is good?') and brings it to a new level of deliberation—'better than'. It is distinct from the previous chapter both in mood and in the manner of speaking. Instead of the somewhat frustrated and probing mood of Qohelet, the collective voice of wisdom speaks in a positive and affirmative tone. Every two-line 'better than' saying has centuries of collective lived experience of the ancient community of Israel to back it up. It is almost like a thin slice of New York cheesecake, not angel cake; it is weighty and heavy stuff. The sayings are meant to edify, to instruct, and the first audience is expected to follow them as normative truths (though in places like vv. 1b, 3, 6a, 8, 10, there is much room left for the audience to ponder). They are non-sophisticated, practical wisdom, delivered in the form of proverbial sayings.

This passage is composed of seven 'better than' sayings (vv. 1 [2x], 2, 3, 5, 8a, 8b) with qualifiers (in parentheses and *italics*) explicating the moral behind. They can be presented below with their respective illustrations:

(1) A good name is   better than   fine perfume (v. 1a)
(2) [And] the day of death is better than   the day of birth (v. 1b)
(3) Going to a house of mourning is better than going to a house of feasting (v. 2a)

(for death is the destiny of everyone,
the living should take this to heart) (v. 2b)

(4) Frustration is   better than   laughter (v. 3a)

(a sad face is good for the heart) (v. 3b)
(The heart of the wise is in the house of mourning,
but the heart of fools is in the house of pleasure.) (v. 4)

(5) Heeding the rebuke of a   better than   listening to the songs of
    wise person is   fools (v. 5b)

(Like the cracking of thorns under the pot,
so is the laughter of fools.)
(Extortion turns a wise person into a fool,
a bribe corrupts the heart.) (v. 6a)

(6) The end of a matter is   better than   its beginning (v. 8a)
(7) Patience is   better than   pride (v. 8b)

Like the other wisdom literature (esp. Proverbs), with the 'heart' as a dominant word (vv. 2, 3, 4 (2x), 7), three key concepts (along with their associated qualifiers) appear in these seven axioms: (1) mourning (sad face, frustration) and feasting (pleasure, laughter, song); (2) death (end of a matter) and living (day of birth, beginning of the matter); (3) wise and fools (extortion, receiving a bribe). Against the ancient domestic society and family life, these three concepts appeal to the first audience as practical wisdom in conducting their lives under the sun.

Considering the seven proverbial sayings, I note the sixth axiom adds further qualification to the first one, which says a good reputation is better than expensive perfume, such as preserving a good name till one dies is better than when a life is just being born. Verse 8 explains further that the end of the matter (when it could be judged) is better than its beginning (with outcomes still unknown). Focusing on mourning and feasting that an average member of the community will experience, the second axiom says outright that going to a house of mourning is better than seeking presence at a place of feasting. Again, v. 2b carries the moral further in stating that death is the final destiny of all humankind, and when pondering the deceased and mourning with the grieving family, the living will take the matter to heart and be reminded. The third axiom (v. 3) and v. 4 follow the 'sadness' and 'heart' motif. A disturbed/discomforting feeling (or a 'sad face') is better than laughter (v. 3a), for a 'sad face' is good for nourishing one's 'heart' (setting the priority of one's conduct of living, v. 3b). Against the didactic context, v. 4 connects the first four axioms with the last three sensibly. On the one hand, it adds more diction to the second axiom regarding the wise choice of being with the mourning family or seeking pleasure in the house of feasting (v. 2). On the other hand, it opens a comparison between the 'heart' of the 'wise' and the 'heart' of fools with two different priorities of conduct. Verses 7 and 8 exemplify the fifth axiom with an analogy (v. 6) and practical advice (v. 8). The analogy is that when one uses thorns instead of wood as fuel for cooking, the thorns make more noise than heat. Therefore, the laughter (pleasing words of the fools) is only noisy but without substance. Verse 7 is a difficult verse in terms of its proper translation (and thus interpretation; cf. Bartholomew 1999: 248-52; Goldingay 2021a: 200-201). 'Extortion/vexation turns a wise person into a fool; and a bribe corrupts the heart'; this saying broadens and extends the contrast between the wise and the fools. Adopting Goldingay's interpretation, it refers to 'being vexed in spirit', which will turn a wise person into a fool. A bribe also corrupts the 'heart', which is an important aspect of wisdom's admonition here (2021a: 200).

Wisdom's voice continues to admonish in the context of being wise or turning to be a fool. The fifth axiom warns that heeding the rebuke (discomforting) of a wise person is better than listening to the song (pleasing words) of fools. The sixth maxim finds its antecedent in v. 7b, 'the end of the matter is better than its beginning', as an indirect summary of wisdom's sayings along the subject of 'death–birth' and 'end–beginning'. Surprisingly, at the end of wisdom's voice giving admonitions in the form of a series of 'better-than' sayings, Qohelet's personal voice bursts out with the *hebel* declaration: 'This too is vanity' (v. 6b)! In essence, this is his own reaction to his *pretext,* the collective voice of wisdom about the hows of conducting one's life. Read in this context, it is quite startling!

The seven 'better than' sayings are followed by wisdom's two instructions ('Do not . . . ,' vv. 9, 10) in praise of 'being wise'. Verse 9 means to have self-control over one's temper ('do not be easily provoked . . . and react with anger'). The second instruction concerns an attitude in life: be forward looking. Do not ask, 'why were the old days better than these?' (v. 10). It is unwise to ask such questions, and it paves the way for wisdom's appeal in vv. 13-14 regarding entrusting ourselves to the order of God's ruling. Verses 11-12 are wisdom's voice in praise of wisdom. Like an inheritance, wisdom is beneficial, a good thing. It is God's gift (v. 11). Using the analogy of a shelter/shadow, as silver/money is a shelter, wisdom provides protection to those who live under the sun. Verses 11-12 can be considered as a continuation of the 'better-than' sayings. The emphasis of v. 12 is not so much on the non-lasting protection that 'wisdom' provides, or the limited privilege that 'money' can benefit those who possess it. Rather, it highlights the permanent benefits of cultivated wisdom and wealth. As Brown notes, 'One comes to possess wisdom as one acquires wealth; both require cultivation' (2000: 78). Verse 12 affirms the true advantage of *experiential knowledge* (cf. Proverbs 1.7, 'knowledge' is consistently used in the Old Testament in the sense of 'experiential knowledge'). '[I]t is smartness that will keep its owner alive' (Goldingay 2021a: 201)! In sum, smartness (practiced/cultivated) wisdom (=*experiential knowledge*) is better than non-enduring protection that one may enjoy (cf. NIV translation implies the same idea—'but the advantage of knowledge is that: Wisdom preserves those who have it'). Reading vv. 11-12 correctly, I believe we must take the repeated use of the word 'wisdom' (3x) as intentional, not intended to frustrate its audience; and v. 12b is meant to refer to wisdom par excellence: the true benefit of wisdom is to give life, to preserve the wise. Not only is wisdom viewed as a beneficial body of knowledge; wisdom also provides direction and the dynamics of life to those who possess it—in setting life's priorities and conducting one's life.

Scholars find that it is difficult to establish the overall coherence of the passage here (see Weeks 2021: 146, Murphy 1992: 61-62). Others seek to force their way in interpreting difficult verses like vv. 7 and 11-12. (I appreciate a lot of Enns's take on the interpretive issues here; cf. 2011: 80-82.) Broadly speaking, I find the sayings in ch. 7 well connected once I have identified its overall structure and the movement of wisdom's admonitions here. Taking Qohelet's outcry in v. 6b as an intentional inclusion amidst wisdom's sayings, I witness the true benefits of reading Ecclesiastes dialogically. Qohelet is responding to his pretext, the collective voice of traditional wisdom with an outburst: 'All is vanity' (v. 6b)! That also sets the tone of his reflection on his life explorations from 7.15 onwards.

2. Wisdom's voice affirming the order of God's ruling (7.13-14)

¹³ *Consider what God has done:*

Who can straighten
  what he has made crooked?
¹⁴ *When times are good, be happy;*
  but when times are bad, consider this:
God has made the one
  as well as the other.
Therefore, no one can discover
  anything about their future.

Using two imperatives ('Consider/look!', vv. 13-14), wisdom's voice urges the first audience to admit the alternation of good and bad times in life as God's order of ruling in their lives. It affirms outrightly with a rhetorical question: 'Who can straighten what God has made crooked?' The expected reflective response from the audience is, 'no one can alter this divinely ordered reality'. It is about submitting to the sovereignty of God in one's life. Wisdom's voice then goes on to encourage the audience to enjoy the good times in life and be happy (v. 14a). When times are bad, 'consider this' (second imperative): 'God has made the one as well as the other' (v. 14a)—a double affirmation. One should accept the bad times in God's order of ruling without any bitterness, as the inevitable difficulties in life under the sun (v. 14b). The passage ends with a quite pessimistic notion: 'Therefore, no one can discover anything about their future' (v. 14c). In a way, this uncertainty is a slice of life's reality. Reading Ecclesiastes narratively and as a memoir, the disheartening thought in v. 14c kicks off another series of Qohelet's first-person explorations of life in 7.15–10.7.

I. Qohelet's First-Person Exploration of Life Continued (7.15–10.7)

1. Seventh cycle of exploration (7.15-18)

Interlude: Second-person wisdom sayings (7.19-22)

¹⁵ *In this meaningless life of mine I have seen both of these:*

  the righteous perishing in their righteousness,
    and the wicked living long in their wickedness.
¹⁶ *Do not be over-righteous,*
    neither be overwise—
    why destroy yourself?

¹⁷ Do not be overwicked,
   and do not be a fool—
   why die before your time?
¹⁸ It is good to grasp the one
   and not let go of the other.
   Whoever fears God will come forth with both of them[16].

Speaking as a memoirist, here Qohelet states overtly the results of his exploration in life with the characteristic motto: 'In the days of my vanity, I have seen . . .' (literally, v. 15a). In the form of a normative statement, he openly declares that in his meaningless life, he has witnessed 'the righteous perishing in their righteousness, and the wicked living long in their wickedness' (v. 15b). 'The wicked enjoying the longevity of life and the righteous perishing in early death' is a complete reversal of the two-way doctrine (Prov. 3.33; Deut. 11:26-28; 28.1, 15) or the blessing-and-cursing principle of God's ruling (after Ps. 1). The strangely negative tone of vv. 16 and 17 is puzzling to many. Some take the three 'do nots' as a continuation of wisdom's instructions in 7.7-12 (cf. Heim 2019: 135). Others focus on the idea of intentional (excessive) human efforts (be wholly faithful and act wisely) to ensure a blessed long life. Goldingay notes, 'the significance of the double prohibition in v. 16 is indicated by the rationale that follows: why be devastated?' (2021a: 207). If we think in this fashion, we will be feeling distraught if things do not turn out in accordance with the order of God's ruling.

The ambiguity in vv. 16-17 can best be understood in the context of Qohelet's emotive response after seeing a repetitive absurd situation in his lifetime (note that he always seeks to respond to his pretext, the traditional wisdom): 'The righteous perishing in their righteousness, and the wicked living long in their wickedness' (v. 15). This is not an isolated case of deviation from the deed-and-consequence principle, but it has cumulative eye-witnesses in the collective lived experience of his community. In a depressive mood, he utters the summary of his observations in the form of two prohibitive rhetorical questions: 'Why destroy yourself?' (v. 16) and 'Why die before your time?' (v. 17). Reading from the perspective of Qohelet's emotive response, the four 'do nots' in vv. 16-17 are not to be understood as instructions or prohibitions. In disillusion and disappointment, Qohelet is letting out his frustration through the emphatic fourfold negations: (1) do not be over-righteous; (2) do not be overwise; (3) do not be overwicked; and (4) do not be a fool. Amid these depressing expressions, Qohelet concludes this cycle of life exploration with some reflective advice: What we must do

---

16. Better translation of the Hebrew.

is 'grasp and not let go of both' (v. 18). To translate this in more practical terms, 'grasping both facts' refers to the following: (a) being over-righteous and overwise will not guarantee long life; and (b) being overwicked and foolish may not lead to longevity of life neither. In a bold statement, Qohelet affirms that 'whoever fears God will avoid all extremes' [literally, 'shall come forth with all of them'] (v. 18). Fearing God can enable us to accept both facts ('a' and 'b') and move on with our lives, and not be destroyed by disappointment.

Reading this passage dialectically and in a 'grain-crossing' fashion, the contradictions and paradoxes embedded in vv. 15-18 take on a new dimension of meaning, especially when 7.15 is put in the broader context of Old Testament teaching (contra, e.g., Prov 3.33; Deut. 11.26-28; ch. 28). 'The righteous gets what the wicked deserve and the wicked gets what the righteous deserves'—this eyewitness situation establishes itself almost as a normative statement alongside Prov. 3.33—'the Lord's blessing is upon the house of the righteousness and his cursing upon the house of the wicked'. Proverbs 3.33 is truth, but in no way can it represent the whole truth about the cause-and-effect principle of God's ruling. Ecclesiastes 7.15-18 does speak loudly in response to traditional wisdom (Qohelet's pretext). It adds a deepened layer of truth to the blessing-and-cursing principle. Fearing God empowers us to embrace both extremes (excessively righteous and overly wise) and be able to move forward, letting go of all the disillusion and frustration that can potentially destroy us. Like the production of plywood (a high-quality, good strength wood panel), reading 'cross the grains' has the potential of yielding a multifaceted, more enriched meaning-significance of this passage.

Ecclesiastes 7.15-18 connects beautifully with the previous chapters in the following ways: *First,* together with 1.15; 3.14-15; 5.7 [MT 6]; and 7.13-14, 7.15-18 ends with the affirmation of God's sovereignty in his order of ruling and the admonition to 'fear God', though at times, amidst delusion and frustration. *Second* is the dynamics of Qohelet's dialogic interaction with the voice of wisdom. Through this momentum, new angles of perception or new dimensions of meaning are opened for us. *Third,* the same subject matters surface in 7.15-18—wise and foolish, righteous and wicked, longevity of life or short-lived life. In most cases, the question one asks will determine the answer one gets. Therefore, it is important to ask good questions of the text. I have been asking the question of coherence throughout this commentary. Thus far, we witness the vibrancy of the different voices engaging in dialogue with one another (that of Qohelet, his inner voice, wisdom's voice, and our readerly voice). I invite all readers to liberate your readerly voice and engage with the different voices ingrained in the text.

Interlude: Second-person wisdom sayings (7.19-22)

*¹⁹ Wisdom makes one wise person more powerful
   than ten rulers in a city.
²⁰ Indeed, there is no one on earth who is righteous,
   no one who does what is right and never sins.
²¹ Do not pay attention to every word people say,
   or you may hear your servant cursing you—
²² for you know in your heart
   that many times you yourself have cursed others.*

As a continuation of Qohelet's reflection on righteousness and wisdom, wisdom's voice joins in praise of the value of wisdom. 'Wisdom makes a wise person more powerful than ten rulers in a city' (v. 19). Wisdom is strength and is immensely powerful, equal to the ruling power of ten rulers. Shifting the focus from wisdom to righteousness (also as a continuation of 7.15-18), wisdom affirms: 'Indeed, there is no one on earth who is righteous, no one who does what is right and never sins' (v. 20). This is a qualifier of the status of a righteous person. Doing what is right does not qualify a person for the claim that he/she is sinless. Using the catchword of the 'heart', wisdom then turns to practical advice in the form of a prohibition—'Do not pay attention to every word people say, so that you may not hear your slave cursing you' (v. 21). Related to v. 20, the advice here is not so much urging the audience to increase their tolerance of the nasty things people would say about them, nor to protect themselves so as not to be hurt by the cursing words that their servants would say about them behind their back. In response to v. 20 ('one who does what is right never sins'), the main purpose of wisdom's advice here is twofold: (1) in their heart (conscience), the audience fully realizes and must accept that they have done the same thing to others (cursing their enemies, v. 22); and (2) they should avoid discomfort to themselves by accepting reality as spelled out in v. 22—in fact, many times they have done the same thing to others (cf. Fox 1999: 263).

2. Eighth cycle of exploration (7.23-26)

²³ All this I tested by wisdom and I said,

'I am determined to be wise' —
   but this was beyond me.
²⁴ Whatever exists is far off and most profound—
   who can discover it?
²⁵ So I turned my mind to understand,
   to investigate and to search out wisdom and the scheme of things

and to understand the stupidity of wickedness
and the madness of folly.
²⁶ I find more bitter than death
the woman who is a snare,
whose heart is a trap
and whose hands are chains.
The man who pleases God will escape her,
but the sinner she will ensnare.

Qohelet the memoirist indicates in this cycle of exploration the strategy of his exploration in life. Reading 7.23-26 as a coherent whole, I agree with Heim that 'all this' (v. 23) refers to the previous explorations instead of the preceding and following investigations (see Heim 2019: 141; also, Enns 2011: 86). Verses 23-24 present an interpretive issue among commentators. 'All this I tested by wisdom, and I said, "I am determined to be wise, but this was beyond me"' (v. 23). The key to interpretation is whether 'wisdom' is the *object* of Qohelet's searching or the *means*. Along with the NIV translation, I opt for seeing wisdom as the *means* instead of the *object* (see Heim, 143 vs. Seow 1997: 252, 259, which implies a failure of his inquiry). 'I said, I am determined to be wise' (an interior monologue) points to the idea that despite his determined efforts, the *object* of his search not only remains beyond his reach, but it continues to be far away (v. 24). The unsearchable outcome is further intensified with a rhetorical question: 'who can discover it?' Up to v. 24, the first audience might think Qohelet has admitted his failure to attain wisdom. Verse 25 continues to focus on the search, and three similar words are used to describe the intensity and intentionality of his search—'So I turned my mind *to understand* (i.e. experiential understanding), *to investigate* and *to search out* wisdom and the 'scheme' of things (other translations: 'calculation of things', Enns 2011: 86; 'accounting', Seow 1997: 260-61; 'sum of things', Longman 1998: 202-203; 'solution of things', Fox 1999: 268). The word 'to understand' is used twice here, implying experiential knowledge rather than head knowledge. Taking 'the scheme/reckoning of things' as the *object* of Qohelet's search ('by wisdom'—as the *means*), v. 25 means 'I had wanted to employ the attained wisdom as my ability to come to an experiential realization of the stupidity of wickedness and the madness of folly'. With wisdom as his pretext, Qohelet goes after the book of Proverbs, using the imagery of the adulterous woman (Prov. 5; 7) as an allusion to personified woman folly (v. 26). He then comes to the realization that the stupidity of wickedness and the madness of folly are more bitter than death. Though an adulterous woman can trap and chain the sinner with evil deeds, the one who pleases God can escape her snare.

3. Ninth cycle of exploration (7.27–8.8)

Interlude: Second-person wisdom sayings (8.1-8)

²⁷ 'Look', **SAYS THE PREACHER (QOHELET)**, 'this is what I have discovered:
Adding one thing to another to discover the scheme of things—
²⁸   while I was still searching
    but not finding—
I found one upright man among a thousand,
    but not one upright woman among them all.
²⁹ "Behold",[17] this only have I found:
    God created mankind upright,
    but they have gone in search of many schemes.'

Joining the dialogic polyphony and thus making his presence known (cf. Longman 1998: 205; Seow 1997: 264), the third-person frame narrator introduces Qohelet's ninth cycle of explorations. Qohelet opens with an astonishing 'behold', signifying an interior monologue and highlighting the sum of his exploration—'this is what I have discovered' (v. 27a). The same Hebrew catchword, 'to seek, to find', appears seven times in vv. 26-29 (vv. 26, 27 [2x], 28 [3x], 29). This frequent occurrence underscores the idea that the focus of Qohelet's exploration is on 'searching'. In keeping with our interpretation of the 'scheme' of things as the *object* of Qohelet's inquiry, vv. 27b and v. 28 spell out the agenda as well as the outcome of the search. The Hebrew word for 'scheme/account' appears only three times in the Hebrew Bible, and it is specifically used only in Ecclesiastes (7.25, 27 and 9.10). 'Adding one to one to find out the sum' (literally v. 27b = full account) is the search agenda, and 'my soul is still seeking, but has not found' is the outcome. Verse 28 elaborates further on the dynamic as well as the result of the search. Qohelet is still searching, but not finding (v. 28a)—'I can only find one upright man among a thousand, but not one upright woman among the upright' (v. 28b). In essence, I think the point here is that Qohelet shares with his audience the fact that he can scarcely find one upright human being among all humankind. With a captivating declaration—'behold!'—v. 29 sums up his finding in the form of an affirmation of the original design of God's creation: 'God created humankind upright, but they have gone (astray) in search of many schemes (literally, great inventions/devices, v. 29; cf. 9.10).

---

17. 'Behold/see', untranslated in NIV.

As I understand the intended message for Qohelet's first audience, I cannot help but ask one question of the text. What is Qohelet trying to address to his contemporary audience (you and me) here? Viable proposals have been made by commentators. Fox sees that Qohelet is speaking of a common human flaw in that we have the tendency to seek answers and make calculations (i.e. the scheme/full account; see Fox 1999: 272); thus he got himself 'all tangled up in calculations' (272). Enns concludes that this section underlines the notion that Qohelet is anticipating a panelist's appeal to Proverbs, which calls for an active search for wisdom, which will be found. In a way, Qohelet was disappointed after the search, and he responded: 'show me, because I do not see it' (Enns 2011: 89). I am leaning toward reading this section as an emotive response of a memoirist. The focus of Qohelet's response is on 'the limits of wisdom'. On the one hand, Qohelet is sharing with his audience the limit of his human ability to figure out the full account/calculation of things. Yet on the other, he laments for the limit of human efforts to run schemes contrary to what God has intended.

Interlude: Second-person wisdom's sayings (8.1-8)

8

¹ Who is like the wise?
Who knows the explanation of things?
A person's wisdom brightens the face
and changes its hard appearance.

² Obey the king's command, I say, because you took an oath before God. ³ Do not be in a hurry to leave the king's presence. Do not stand up for a bad cause, for he will do whatever he pleases. ⁴ Since a king's word is supreme, who can say to him, 'What are you doing?'

⁵ Whoever obeys his command will come to no harm,
   and the wise heart will know the proper time and procedure.
⁶ For there is a proper time and procedure for every matter,
   though a person may be weighed down by misery.
⁷ Since no one knows the future,
   who can tell someone else what is to come?
⁸ As no one has power over the wind to contain it,
   so no one has power over the time of their death.
 As no one is discharged in time of war,
   so wickedness will not release those who practice it.

Reading Ecclesiastes polyphonically, it makes no difference if 8.1 serves as a conclusion to 7.27-29 (most commentators; see Enns 2011: 89) or introduces 8.2-8. Following the same chain of Qohelet's thoughts on the *object* and *outcome* of his search, wisdom speaks out in 8.1. Deftly employing two rhetorical questions, wisdom's voice first extols the value of wisdom ('Who is like the wise?') and then affirms its 'limit' ('who knows the explanation of things?'). As an extended appraisal of wisdom, 8.1b says, 'A person's wisdom brightens the face, and changes its hard appearance'. This interlude of wisdom's sayings connects 7.26-29 and 8.2-8 coherently as a dialogue between traditional wisdom and the explorer, Qohelet.

Qohelet's I-voice continues in 8.2-8. Following wisdom's instructional tone of speaking ('Do not be in a hurry to leave the king's presence. Do not stand up for a bad cause … , v. 3), he turns to another subject of discussion—submitting to the king's command and authority as an oath one made before God (v. 2). Indeed, reverent obedience to the king is part of traditional wisdom's teaching (Prov. 24.21), and people are not supposed to exalt themselves in the king's presence (Prov. 25.6). With traditional wisdom as his pretext, Qohelet further affirms that the king's word is supreme beyond any challenge (v. 4). He then moves to the issue of the 'right time' in vv. 5-6. Obeying the king's command is a protection, but it is conditioned by a 'discerning, wise heart' to know the proper time and procedure (see Fox 1999: 278-79). Despite a person's being weighed down by misery, one must decide 'what to do when'. Verses 5 and 6 reinforce what wisdom's voice affirms in 3.1-11.

Verses 7-8 depart from the topic of human control to emphasize humanity's ignorance of the right times and uncertainty of the future—'Since no one knows the future, who can tell someone else what is to come?' (v. 7). Heim notes that five negatives are used in vv. 7- 8: (a) 'no one knows the future'; (b) 'no one has power over the wind'; (c) 'no one has power over the time of their death'; (d) 'no one is discharged in time of war; and (e) 'wickedness will not release its possessors' (cf. Heim 2019: 152). The five negations together accentuate what humanity cannot control—that is, the limits inherent in human power (see Fox 1999: 274).

On the surface, 8.1-8 moves from obeying the king's supreme power to the demand for humans to judge 'what to do when', then proceeds to the limit of human control (more precisely, the limit of human wisdom). This section correlates with the previous chapters on certain strategic junctions: for example, God's order of creation (3.1-8); God's sovereignty in running human lives (3.14-15); and the value of wisdom and being wise (4.13). I see it is possible that Qohelet's response to traditional wisdom here is also an allusion to the supreme power, the sovereignty of God (see 5.1-7 [MT 4.17–5.6]). To the first audience, it makes much sense as they listen to Qohelet moving from the 'do not sayings' (vv. 2-5a) to the issue of knowing the proper time and procedure; then he goes deeper to the uncertainty about the future and the time of one's death (vv. 5b-8).

William Murphy observes a 'dialectic' between Qohelet and traditional wisdom all through this section (extending to 8.16). To him, Qohelet's narration in vv. 2-4 belongs to traditional court wisdom. He is not simply transmitting a body of sayings with his I-voice. 'He is relativizing the role and prestige of the sage (v. 1) by following up with (wise!) admonitions that in fact are humiliating for the sage at court . . .' (see Murphy 1992: 82-83). The wise sages are confronted by royal power and are totally dependent on the king's pleasure. Perceiving Qohelet's instructions in vv. 2-4 (which are in fact derived from traditional wisdom) serves to qualify v. 1; he is undoubtedly in dialectic with his pretext, traditional wisdom. To Murphy, Qohelet 'pits traditional wisdom against itself' (83).

As one of the reading strategies employed in this commentary, 'reading Ecclesiastes dialectically' has the potential for understanding the book from another angle of perception, as demonstrated above. Employing the same reading strategy would be beneficial to readers as we move on to the later chapters.

4. *Tenth cycle of exploration (8.9-13)*
Reflective summary: On fearing God (8.12-13)

[9] All this I saw, as I applied my mind to everything done under the sun. There is a time when people lord it over others to their own hurts. [10] Then I saw the wicked buried. They used to come and go from the holy place! But those were forgotten in the city who had acted justly. This also is meaningless.[18]

[11] When the sentence for a crime is not quickly carried out, people's hearts are filled with schemes to do wrong. [12] Although a wicked person who commits a hundred crimes may live a long time, I know that it will go better with those who fear God, who are reverent before him. [13] Yet because the wicked do not fear God, it will not go well with them, and their days will not lengthen like a shadow.

'All this' (v. 9a) may refer to all the things Qohelet has witnessed thus far (from the first to the ninth cycles of exploration). The intentionality of his exploration is stated in v. 9b, 'as I applied my mind to everything under the sun'. Verse 9c is ambiguous; it may refer to 'those who are subject to human authority are harmed' (Fox 1999: 282), or alternatively, the ruling powers may harm themselves (Crenshaw 1987: 153). If v. 9 is understood in

---

18. I follow Roland Murphy's translation of this difficult verse (Murphy 1992:79).

this way, it may serve as a connecting verse, a short conclusion to 8.1-8, or an introduction to the following sections (8.10-12).

Qohelet now turns to two other specific cases that have been carefully observed (i.e. witnessed and brought to heart, vv. 9 a and b), both related to the apparent injustice in God's order of ruling. Verse 10 reads: 'Then I saw the wicked buried. They used to come and go from the holy places! But those were forgotten in the city who had acted justly. This too is vanity! (I favor Murphy's translation for this ambiguous verse; see Murphy 1992: 79). *First,* Qohelet points out an ironic case: the wicked (who themselves used to go about the holy places) received proper burial (as a reward, a blessed outcome for the just in the Hebrew mind), but the righteous were forgotten in the city. This is followed by another reflective observation, 'when the sentence of a crime is not carried out, people's hearts are filled with schemes (v. 11; see discussion in 7.25, 29). *Second,* because of the situation described in v. 11, nothing can stop a wicked person committing a hundred crimes from still enjoying longevity of life (v. 12a). Again, longevity of life is a sign of blessedness granted by God in accordance with the blessing-and-cursing principle, the order of God's ruling (cf. Prov. 3.2, 13-17; 10.27).

Reflective summary: On fearing God (8.12-13)

After his lamenting outcry in v. 10, Qohelet now turns to an affirmation as his reflective summary of his explorations in life. Qohelet never denies the blessing-and-cursing principle (Deut. 11.26-28; Prov. 3.33). The 'although' in v. 12 underscores the declaration in v. 12b '. . . I *know* it is better with those who fear God, those who are reverent before him' (5.7 [MT 6]; 7.18). Verse 13 further extends and adds diction to his assertion. Since the wicked do not fear God, the long lives which they apparently enjoy will not go well with them. Without the sustenance of God, humanity cannot endure just like shadow does not sustain (v. 13).

5. *Eleventh cycle of exploration (8.14)*

[14] There is something else of vanity that occurs on earth: the righteous who get what the wicked deserve, and the wicked who get what the righteous deserve. This too, I say, is vanity.

In the form of a report of his observation, 8.14 is a powerful summary appraisal of the memoirist Qohelet. It is positioned at the centre of the book of Ecclesiastes. The double appearance of *hebel* in this verse intensifies the weight of this assessment: There is a *hebel* that occurs on earth—'the righteous get what the wicked deserve, and the wicked get what the righteous deserve'. This observed reality presents a complete reversal of the two-way (blessing-and-cursing) principle, God's order of ruling. In his 'I'-voice, Qohelet bravely admits that this is indeed *hebel*! To the contemporary mind, this setback is a slice of life's reality, almost as a normality of our collective lived experience under the sun. However, against Qohelet's pretext—traditional wisdom (e.g. Prov. 3.33)—it is rather extraordinary for him to declare this summary of his exploration in life. In a way, his lived experience is in dialectic with his belief, which is rooted in the teachings of traditional wisdom. Reading Ecclesiastes polyphonically and dialectically can guide readers to appreciate the presence of different competing voices engaging in vigorous dialogues (in this case, between Qohelet and traditional wisdom), yielding the result of detecting the dialectics engrained in the text (i.e. the complete reversal of the reward for the righteous and the wicked).

6. *Fifth* carpe diem *saying (8.15)*

¹⁵ So I commend the enjoyment of life, because there is nothing better for a person under the sun than to eat and drink and be glad. Then joy will accompany them in their toil all the days of the life God has given them under the sun.

As commentators have pointed out (see Goldingay 2021: 207; Fox 1999: 287), the appearance of Qohelet's fifth *carpe diem* saying after the declaration in 8.14 is shocking to his audience. Verse 15 begins with 'So . . .'. It indicates that because of the dialectic situation as depicted in 8.12-14, Qohelet recommends the enjoyment of life—there is nothing better for a person under the sun than to eat, drink and be glad. Both Goldingay and Fox see that this praise of enjoyment may serve as a *diversion* in coping with the 'toil' of life. Goldingay specifically comments on the fact that Qohelet embraces and affirms both realities: the two-way principle spelled out in Psalm 1; Deut. 11.26-28; Prov. 3.33, and the dialectic created in 8.12-14 (cf. Pss. 73; 44). As Lee has noted, the conventional truth is held on an equal plane with the contradictory cases cited around it (vv. 9-14). In embracing the coexisting dialectic tensions in life, v. 15 serves as a *distraction* for Qohelet's audience. I find this *carpe diem* saying very much in line with the diction of the previous ones. It is a positive affirmation of the 'joy' amidst tensions which God has promised to accompany them 'in their toil all the days of the life God has given them under the sun' (literally, v. 15b). If we take 'toil' in a broader sense (i.e. work), not with a negative connotation as 'the burden of life', then I think the point affirmed by Qohelet is 'enjoyment in life is part of the divine design' for living our lives under the sun. It is *not* a diversion, but *the* way of *'how to live!'* Lee further notes, the particulars of the good life are: (There is nothing better than) to eat, drink

7. Twelfth cycle of exploration (8.16-17)

¹⁶ When I applied my mind to know wisdom and to observe the labor that is done on earth—people getting no sleep day or night— ¹⁷ then I saw all that God has done. No one can comprehend what goes on under the sun. Despite all their efforts to search it out, no one can discover its meaning. Even if the wise claim they know, they cannot really comprehend it.

This twelfth cycle of exploration may serve as a general summary of all Qohelet's explorations. The attitude, manner, intensity and outcome of the search are given a flourish in this short episode. The memoirist attests to the fact that he has paid due attention ('when I applied my mind') to gaining 'wisdom' through observing the events that happened on earth—identifying himself with the others who are searching. Gaining wisdom may demand people losing sleep all day and night (v. 16). Verse 17 gives the outcome of the search—a total mystery of the working of God in human lives. 'Then I saw' highlights the firsthand witness, not a hypothetical case study. No one can comprehend what is going on under the sun. Despite all human intentional efforts (to pay attention, to observe and reflect on the happenings day and night, to the extent of losing sleep, v. 16b), still the path of God's working is beyond human comprehension. The incomprehensibility of God despite the intentional and intensive searching of humans is the assertion here.

8. Thirteenth cycle of exploration (9.1-2)

9

¹ Indeed,[19] all this I took to my heart even to examine all this.[20] The righteous and the wise and what they do are in God's hands, but no one knows whether love or hate awaits them. ² All share a common destiny—the righteous and the wicked, the good and the bad, the clean and the unclean, those who offer sacrifices and those who do not.

> As it is with the good,
>   so with the sinful;
> as it is with those who take oaths,
>   so with those who are afraid to take them.

---

19. A more forceful translation.
20. A literal translation.

'Indeed, all this I took to my heart even to examine all this' (v. 1). This thirteenth cycle of exploration can be regarded as a cumulative summary appraisal of Qohelet's previous twelve explorations. In keeping with the characteristic polar structure of the book, seven sets of antithetical designations are presented. They can be regarded as moral, religious and intellectual human qualities: (1) love–hatred; (2) the righteous–the wicked; (3) the good–the bad; (4) the clean–the unclean; (5) those who regularly offer sacrifice–those who do not; (6) the good–the sinful; and (7) those who utter oaths–those who are afraid to take oaths. Rooted in traditional wisdom thinking, Qohelet's category of humanity's conduct and worship life before God is divided basically into two: the righteous (those who do good and abide in love, offering sacrifice [cf. 5.1, MT 4.17], and fulfilling the oaths pledged to God [cf. 5.4-5, MT 5.3-4]) and the wicked (those who do bad and abide in hatred, failing to fulfil oaths and offer sacrifice). The plethora of contrasting descriptions here points to the fact that Qohelet sees that one's character will naturally reflect one's conduct and attitude before God. One's moral character and acts emerging from that character are consistent.

With traditional wisdom as Qohelet's pretext, the rhetorical effects in vv. 1-2 present a sharp irony. Qohelet brings out two elements in his reflective conclusion: *First,* even for the righteous and the wise (who do good and remain faithful; those who have the intellectual quality), all their acts are in God's hands. They will face the same *uncertainty* of their future ('if love or hate awaits them', v. 1b). I concur with Goldingay that according to Mal. 1.2-3, the 'love' or 'hate' here may refer to the two contrasting outcomes of God's response to human actions (2021a: 236). *Second,* echoing 7.13-14, the righteous (good) and the wicked (sinful) all share an undiscriminating common destiny (v. 2). Moreover, v. 1b reinforces his concluding statement in 8.16-17. Despite the human efforts to search God's order of things, it remains unfathomable (cf. 3.8; 8.17). Brown notes here that Qohelet considers this situation of human indeterminacy and the incomprehensibility of God's order a *travesty* (2000: 91). The fate of all is the same no matter who or what they are or how they conduct their lives.

Chapter 9 begins literally, 'For all this, I took to my heart' (v. 1a). Qohelet's concluding 'reflection' emerges from an activity in his heart. Many agree that 'heart' is the seat of intellect and will in the Hebrew mentality. Yet, 'heart' is also the locus of the description of many emotional states in the Old Testament, expressing strong emotions of joy (Pss. 4.8 [MT 7]; 13.6 [MT 5]; 16.9; 9.2 [MT 1]) and grief (Pss. 13.3 [MT 2]; 34.19 [MT 18]; 51.17 [MT 16]; 147.3; Isa. 61.1; Jer. 4.19; Hos. 11.8; cf. also Smith 1998: 427-36).

Noting this dimension is important in reading Ecclesiastes as a memoir. Qohelet's reflective summary of his observations in life shared thus far are emotion laden. His distress from here on abounds.

9. Fourteenth cycle of exploration (9.3-6)

³ This is the evil in everything that happens under the sun: The same destiny overtakes all. The hearts of people, moreover, are full of evil and there is madness in their hearts while they live, and afterward they join the dead. ⁴ Anyone, who is among the living, has hope—even a live dog is better off than a dead lion!

⁵ For the living know that they will die,
    but the dead know nothing;
  they have no further reward,
    and even their name is forgotten[21].
⁶ Their love, their hate
    and their jealousy have long since vanished;
  never again will they have a part
    in anything that happens under the sun.

In this cycle of exploration, Qohelet moves from his observation of humanity's coping with the unpredictability of the future (9.1b) to the absurd reality of the indiscriminating fate of death which overtakes all—the righteous and the wicked (9.2-3). Both Krüger (2004: 170) and Heim (2019: 163) consider v. 3 as an allusion to Gen. 6.5 ('Yahweh saw how great the wickedness of the human race had become on earth, and that every imagination of the thoughts of the human heart was only evil all the time'; cf. Gen. 3.19). In this sense, the 'evil' referred to in v. 3 goes back to the wickedness of the generation of Genesis 1–11, with the common destiny of the death of all people as God's judgment. This view is a theological overtone in the immediate context of a reflective deliberation; Qohelet's pessimistic outlook in life is at its climax—since 'everything is still in God's hands' (9.1).

Underscoring the common destiny of death, v. 3 serves as a crucial link connecting vv. 1-2 with vv. 4-6. It is regarded as a cumulative outcome of Qohelet's explorations in life. Ecclesiastes 9.1-2 underscores the fate of death indiscriminately to the good and the bad, the righteous and the wicked, the clean and the unclean, those who offer sacrifices and those who do not, those who take oaths and those who are afraid to do so. In v. 3,

---

21. Literally, 'for their memory is forgotten'.

Qohelet depicts 'evil' as an undifferentiating 'situation'—('This is the evil in *everything* that happens *under the sun*'), in that the *same* fate of death overtakes *all* humanity, irrespective of their conduct and actions. Heart is the seat of intelligence, will and emotion in the Hebrew mentality. Focusing on the heart, Qohelet observes that hearts are full of evil and madness while humans are still living. However, one *reality* stands out—all humanity will join the dead afterwards. The power behind Qohelet's articulation in 9.1-6 is captivating. It highlights the irony and ambivalence as shared in Qohelet's concluding reflection. Two trajectories of thought are presented here. *First*, he moves from the 'unpredictability' of human life (9.1) to the 'certainty' of death as a final destiny of all people (9.2-3). *Second*, he reveals a hidden irony. Though the hearts of people are full of evil and madness while they live (v. 3), he praises life over death in vv. 4-6. In a bold statement, Qohelet asserts that 'anyone who is among the living has hope—even a live dog is better off than a dead lion!' As Goldingay notes, 'few creatures are more looked down on than dogs . . . and few creatures are more esteemed than lions' (2021a: 238; cf. 1 Sam. 17.43; Num. 23.24; Judg. 14.18). This is an astonishing and sharp contrast.

In the context of a reflective conclusion, 'This is the "evil" in everything under the sun: The same destiny (of death) overtakes all'. The 'evil' here refers to the *situation* of indiscrimination, undifferentiation between the seven antithetical groups of people (9.1-2). Yet, since the hearts of all people are full of evil and madness while they live, the undifferentiated *situation* of their final destiny is justified in accordance with the two-way doctrine. With Qohelet's negative view of death, he praises life instead (9.4-6). Thus, the depiction in vv. 4-6 intensifies the irony in this cycle of exploration.

Verses 5b-6 paint a sharp contrast between the living and the dead. Qohelet points out the superiority of living in that there is ground for hope and consciousness, which enables one to live properly (v. 5b; Krüger 2004: 170). Yet on the other hand, he asserts that death is gloomy and hopeless. In death, there is no consciousness to seek for further rewards, and, thus, all influences of death upon the world are denied (Heim 2019: 164). Moreover, all emotions perish, and death erases memory (vv. 5b-6; cf. Sun 2017: 185). Precisely, death ushers in the state of 'nothingness' (the 'doing' and 'being' of all humanity; cf. 9.10: 'for in the realm of the dead, . . . there is neither working nor planning nor knowledge nor wisdom'). I see 9.3-6 as the most depressing reflection on Qohelet's exploration of life. Viewing it from the perspective of a memoirist, his emotion is at an utterly distressed climax yet expressed subtly—he is in agony. This paves the way for a startling transition—the sixth *carpe diem* saying (9.7-10).

10. Sixth *carpe diem saying (9.7-10)*

⁷ Go, eat your food with gladness, and drink your wine with a joyful heart, for God has already approved what you do. ⁸ Always be clothed in white, and always anoint your head with oil. ⁹ Enjoy life with your wife, whom you love, all the days of your life of vanity[22] that God has given you under the sun—all your meaningless days/days of vanity.[23] For this is your lot in life and in your toilsome labor under the sun. ¹⁰ Whatever your hand finds to do, do it with all your might, for in the realm of the dead, where you are going, there is neither working nor planning nor knowledge nor wisdom.

This sixth *carpe diem* saying is the most exuberant and elaborate endorsement of enjoyment thus far. As many have noted, it is the first among the seven that involves the use of imperatives (Goldingay 2021a: 239; Lee 2005: 62). Lee further underscores that the movement from Qohelet's indicative and reflective 'I'-narration to the imperative mood and jussives in vv. 7-10 is astonishing. There are seven imperatives in four verses: Go, eat, drink, let them be white, let it not be lacking, enjoy life, act! (63). Together with the use of jussives ('let your garments be white', 'let your head not be lacking oil', v. 8), it is Qohelet's participatory, high-spirited, and most effective way of making his appeal. Moving away from his pessimistic 'I'-voice reflecting on the outcome of death, Qohelet is challenging his audience with an upbeat and enthusiastic charge for them to enjoy life fully with what God has given and approved for them to enjoy.

Verses 7-9 present an anatomy of enjoyment, a sumptuous description with concrete activities that together make up a comprehensive picture of joy. Along with the same theme of enjoyment in life, the specific textual design and thought development in this *carpe diem* saying is worth noting. *First,* the force behind the seven imperatives in this pericope with the jussive mood, on the one hand, underscores the urgency of the encouragement. On the other hand, it minimizes the top-down deliberation of this charge but highlights the idea of mutual encouragement (e.g. 'let us always be clothed in white and let us always anoint our head with oil . . .', v. 8).

Second, v. 7, 'Eat your food with gladness and drink your wine with a joyful heart', points to the manner of consumption as well as the pursuit of happiness (Heim 2019: 165). The significance is found in v. 7b: 'For God has already approved what you do'. This endorsement from God is relevant, as it is the basis for human consciousness and appreciation of the simple but good things in life (food and drink) as gifts from a generous

---

22. Literally, 'life of vanity'.
23. Literally, 'days of vanity'.

God. Qohelet is not merely encouraging self-indulged enjoyment in life but rather *contentment*. Moreover, Qohelet urges his audience to wear a white garment 'all the time' and anoint one's head with oil as symbols for the more lavish, festive way of God's provision (Enns 2011: 96; cf. Ps. 104.15). Verse 9b also states: 'For this is your "lot" in life that God has given you'. Acknowledgment of this 'lot' as the God-allotted 'portion' to humanity is significant, and the response of contentment and 'seizing the day with vigour' is expected.

Third, as Lee has noted, the 'lot/portion' used in v. 9b refers to something more concrete and specific. The overloaded use of second-person pronouns in vv. 7-10 (e.g. your bread, your wine, your works, your garments, etc.) designates what God has given to the human agent for you to enjoy. Thus 'Qohelet underscores the importance of human agency in his ethic of joy' (Lee 2005: 69). The idea of stewardship and human cultivation through all these means is indicated here. Apparently, the empowerment for the human agent here appears to be only self-oriented within one's household (see discussion on 11.1).

Fourth, a dialectic tension is created as Qohelet continues the content of his advice in v. 9. He turns to the domestic dimension and commends his audience to enjoy life with one's wife. The repeated mention of 'all the days of your life of vanity which God has given to you under the sun'—'all the days of your vanity' (v. 9a) is noteworthy. This pessimistic notion amidst a high-spirited appeal of enjoyment in life is puzzling. Again, the locus of our understanding is in v. 9b. Affirming the happiness of family life as one's 'lot' given by God during the days of human labor under the sun is the foundation of this appeal. Amidst the toilsome labor and absurdity in life, yet there is still an urgent call to 'seize the day' and seek enjoyment in the domestic realm. If we read Ecclesiastes dialectically, we can expect the presence of irony within the twelve chapters. Readers are faced with two interpretive options: (1) accept the text as difficult while trying to do our best to interpret the 'contradictions' (as Fox outrightly affirms; cf. Fox 1999: 1-11; Krüger 2004: 171-72; Heim 2019: 166); (2) take the two appearances of 'vanity' in life under the sun as the context to highlight the need, vigour and diction of seeking enjoyment within the family—one dimension of 'seizing the day'. Regardless of the absurdity and vanity of life, Qohelet issues a powerful appeal to his audience to seize the day for life's enjoyment.

Fifth, Qohelet's urge to 'seize the day' calls for commitment –'Whatever your hand finds to do, do it with all your might' (v. 10a). 'Seizing the day' demands vigorous action and self-engagement to seek enjoyment in life by capturing all opportune times that are within the boundary of God's allotted 'portion' and gifts. Also, joy and labor go hand in hand. Verse 10b further intensifies the urgency of 'seizing the day': 'For in the realm of the dead, where you are going, there is neither working, nor planning, nor knowledge, nor wisdom'. This episode exhibits a dramatic movement from the contemplation of death to the reaffirmation of the joy in life. Moreover, as Lee has observed, the use of 'to find' is noteworthy considering Qohelet's repeated emphasis that mortals 'cannot find' the things they seek (3.11; 7.14, 24-28; 8.17 [3 x]; [2005: 67]). Thus in 9.7-10, the appeal 'to find' overturns the frustration of 'not finding' in the rest of the book. A 'cross-graining' reading of this pericope will further enhance the meaning-significance of Ecclesiastes, as in 3.6a, 'A time to seek and a time to give up seeking'. The 'not finding' in 3.11; 7.14, 24-28; 8.17 are truths, but in no way can they represent the whole truth in the context of wisdom. Considering 9.7-10 (esp. v. 10) alongside the rest of the book, readers are impacted with a more holistic teaching on 'finding' through Qohelet's narrations.

11. Fifteenth cycle of exploration (9.11-12)

¹¹ I returned and saw[24] under the sun:

> The race is not to the swift
> or the battle to the strong,
> nor does food come to the wise
> or wealth to the brilliant
> or favor to the learned;
> but time and chance happen to them all.

¹² Moreover, no one knows when their hour will come:

> As fish are caught in a cruel net,
> or birds are taken in a snare,
> so people are trapped by evil times
> that fall unexpectedly upon them.

Verse 11, 'I turned/returned and saw', signifies a new cycle of reflective observation. Reading Ecclesiastes narratively entails taking a view of vv. 11-12 as Qohelet's personal eyewitness and not a hypothetical case study. On the surface, this reflection on life comes quite unnaturally with another change of mood after the most spirited *carpe diem* saying. Yet to Qohelet, the notion of absurdity permeates his reflections. Again, using the rhetoric of negation, he spells out the nonconstant unpredictability of human life under the sun. There is no guaranteed reward/privilege for

---

24. Literally, 'I returned/turned and saw'; the stress here is on the idea of a 180-degree 'turning'.

the swift to win the race, nor for the strong to win the battle. Being wise, brilliant and skillful does not bring you good rewards in life: abundance, wealth and privileges (v. 11). As with the universal fate of death, 'evil' time (v. 13b) and chance happen to all indiscriminately.

Returning to the thought of 'do not know' (which was just overturned in his previous *carpe diem* saying), he states emphatically that 'moreover', 'no one knows when their hour will come' (v. 13). Using an analysis of a fish being caught in a net and birds taken in a snare, 'so people are trapped by evil times that fall upon them unexpectedly'. Hearing Qohelet's 'I'-voice from the perspective of a memoirist, this short cycle of reflection is deep and emotion laden. It serves as a cumulative summary of his lament over the uncertainty and unpredictability of human life. He spells out especially what is deeply engrained in his motto cry: 'Vanity of vanities. All is vanity!' As Enns has rightly commented, Qohelet ends this reflection with a 'sad—indeed crippling—realization' that any 'act of defiance will get you nowhere' (2011: 97)!

12. Sixteenth cycle of exploration (9.13-16)

Interlude: Second-person wisdom sayings (9.7–10.4)

¹³ I also saw under the sun this example of wisdom that greatly impressed me: ¹⁴ There was once a small city with only a few people in it. And a powerful king came against it, surrounded it and built huge siege works against it. ¹⁵ Now there lived in that city a man poor but wise, and he saved the city by his wisdom. But nobody remembered that poor man. ¹⁶ *So I said, 'Wisdom is better than strength'.* But the poor man's wisdom is despised, and his words are no longer heeded.

Qohelet moves on to another reflection on his exploration, and he shares with his audience that it is an example of 'wisdom' that has greatly impressed him (v. 13). Qohelet presents a case full of dialectic tension. By 'wisdom', a poor but wise man saved a small city from the destruction of a powerful foreign king (vv. 14-15). But afterwards, no one remembered the good deeds of the poor man. Qohelet then turns to his inner self (his inner voice in v. 16a) and affirms that 'wisdom is (still) better than strength' (a reference to the powerful king in v. 14b). Yet, the punch of his reflection is stated in v. 16b—'But the poor man's wisdom is despised, and his words are no longer heeded'. The audience hears the silent and yet bubbling voice of Qohelet: 'What then is the value/reward of wisdom' (v. 16b)! Reading 9.13-16 dialectically opens for us a window to uncover the deep-rooted emotion carried in the 'I'-narration of Qohelet. By citing this eyewitness example, Qohelet is, in effect, responding dialectically and forcefully to his pretext: traditional wisdom in which 'the poor man's wisdom to save a city' is regarded as of high value.

Interlude: Wisdom is indeed better than folly (9.17–10.4)

[17] *The quiet words of the wise are more to be heeded*
than the shouts of a ruler of fools.
[18] *Wisdom is better than weapons of war,*
but one sinner destroys much good.

10

[1] *As dead flies give perfume a bad smell,*
so a little folly outweighs wisdom and honor.
[2] *The heart of the wise inclines to the right,*
but the heart of the fool to the left.
[3] *Even as fools walk along the road,*
they lack sense
and show everyone how stupid they are.
[4] *If a ruler's anger rises against you,*
do not leave your post;
calmness can lay great offenses to rest.

Wisdom's voice joins in at this junction after Qohelet's frustrated response to the value of wisdom. The notion of despair is found in Qohelet's reflection in 9.13-16. Enns sees that the significance of 9.17–10.25 marks a separate section in affirming that 'wisdom really is better than folly' (Enns 2011: 98). Wisdom's voice now speaks authentically and compellingly in response to the 'I'-narration of Qohelet, playing a front stage role in this polyphony.

Wisdom's speech is relatively short but powerful. It seeks to caution the audience to practice vigilance and self-control (Heim 2019: 173). Picking up on some of the themes in previous narrations, wisdom's voice touches on four main areas. *First*, in the form of two 'better than' proverbial sayings, 'the quiet word of the wise' is compared to the 'shouts of the ruler of fools' in a high-pitched manner. The next comparison, 'wisdom is better than weapons of war', again sharpens the contrast (9.17a). *Second*, the penetrating destructive effect of folly is depicted here as 'one act of folly (one sinner) destroys much good' (9.18b). As dead flies destroy the fragrance of perfume, so a little foolish act can potentially outweigh wisdom and honour (10.1). *Third*, the wise and the fools choose different paths in life. The contrast of 'the heart of the wise inclines to the right and the heart of the fools to the left' creates some ambiguity and thus opens to polyvalent interpretation among readers. While Krüger regards 'right' as 'good fortune' and 'left' as 'bad fortune' (cf. 2004: 180), Fox thinks that since 'fools' heart wanders off and turns "left", it signifies fools' incapacity to thinking straight as they wander off the "right" path' (see Fox 1999: 302). I see that the contrast here focuses on the two paths undertaken by the wise and the fools. It highlights the fools' wandering off from the right path as they have no sense of the right direction. Their foolish acts are recognized by everyone (10.2). *Fourth,* wisdom offers powerful practical advice. Against the setting of life of Qohelet's audience (i.e. facing the harshness of foreign rule), wisdom's wise words are quiet, yet powerfully addressed in the form of practical advice: 'If a ruler's anger rises against you, do not leave your post/do not give up' (10.4a). The prevailing word of true wisdom is 'calmness can lay great offenses to rest' (v. 4b). In praise of the antithetic superiority of wisdom against folly, wisdom's speech here depicts wisdom as 'good', the 'fragrant aroma of perfume', 'capable of endowing one with good direction in life' and with 'the quality of calmness which is more powerful than the weapons of war'. This is quite an outstanding depiction of the value of wisdom! The strategic role of the voice of wisdom at this junction is powerfully brought to the foreground.

13. *Seventeenth cycle of exploration (10.5-7)*

5 There is an evil I have seen under the sun,
    the sort of error that arises from a ruler:
6 Fools are put in many high positions,
    while the rich occupy the low ones.
7 I have seen slaves on horseback,
    while princes go on foot like slaves.

The sentiment of despair continues to surface in the foreground in Qohelet's last exploration of life. As 'empirical' examples ('I have seen' [vv. 5a, 7a]), he refers to two eyewitness cases as 'evil' ('There is an "evil" I have seen under the sun', v. 5a) and specifies that they belong to the sort of error that arises from the decision of a ruler (v. 5b). Qohelet describes the 'evil' in vv. 6 and 7 as 'disorderly' in two specific observations: (1) 'fools are put in high positions, but the wealthy occupy the low ones' (v. 6); and (2) slaves travel on horseback while princes go on foot like slaves (v. 7). In the context of Qohelet's life exploration, he apparently is not only depicting a chaotic situation that he has witnessed in society, but he is lamenting the limits of wisdom in turning the disordered situation back to God's 'order of ruling' in human life under the sun. His search for the 'order of things' seems to reach a dead end. Up to 10.5-7, there is no resolution toward the end of his reflection on his exploration in life. Qohelet's reflective 'I'-voice stops here, and the next and the last time he speaks is in the form of an agonizing cry: 'Vanity of vanities! All is vanity!' (12.8). This lamenting cry can be taken as the grand finale summary appraisal of all his experience and explorations before the epilogist speaks authoritatively in 12.9-14. In view of this textual movement, I see what is between 10.7 and 12.8 as vital in this interpretive task. The presence of the different voices at strategic places from 10.8 to 12.14 is the crux toward making some sense of this paradoxical book. I shall guide our readers to put each of the speaking voices on the front stage of our interpretation with focus on their significance at crucial places. The order of the pronouncement of these voices from 10.7 onwards are the second-person voice of wisdom (10.8–12.7); Qohelet's 'I'-voice in the form of a lamenting outcry (12.8a, c); the voice of the frame narrator (12.8b); and the voice of the epilogist (12.9-14). Except for the 'inner voice' of Qohelet, all voices in this polyphonic book are represented in the last three chapters of Ecclesiastes. They dialogue vibrantly and dialectically among themselves and should have significant impact on the original audience as well as readers of today.

J. Second-Person Wisdom Sayings (10.8-12.7)

This section comprises a long list of proverbial sayings, and wisdom's voice speaks with an authoritative voice addressing the audience directly. Commentators differ quite significantly in their treatment of the way that this lengthy wisdom's speech is incorporated into the book. Murphy and Crenshaw left it unexplained (Murphy 1992; Crenshaw 1987), while some opt for taking it as practical advice in life in view of the uncertainties and risks (cf. Seow 1997; Bartholomew 2009; Weeks 2021; Enns 2011; and Heim 2019). In most cases, the question you ask will determine the answer you get. My reading will pay due attention to the flow of textual movement. I will sharply focus on the strength and limit of wisdom, which may potentially lead to Qohelet's grand finale outcry in 12.8 (cf. the approach of Krüger 2004; Goldingay 2021a).

Heim has noted, if this long segment (10.8–12.7) is taken in isolation from the political context, it becomes an obscure insertion in the book (2019). He anchors his approach to interpretation of this episode against the background of a foreign regime and the subtle resistance of the Jewish people. Wisdom's speech in 10.8–12.7 is composed primarily of proverbial sayings (e.g. 10.8-20), instructions and admonitions (e.g. 11.1, 6; the *carpe diem* saying in 11.9-10) and poetic materials (11.2-5). It entails an interpretive strategy that focuses on the significance of its position in the text and the various genres represented in the episode. Moreover, with a polyphonic approach to interpretation, my inquiry will sharply focus on the presence of the voice of wisdom, Qohelet, and the frame narrator—before the epilogist speaks out in the conclusion.

An overview of my approach in this section is reflected in the following outline. *First,* wisdom's voice in 10.8-20 reaffirms that wisdom is indeed better than folly. *Second,* wisdom provides practical advice for life in view of the uncertainties of the risky future (11.1-8). *Third,* in the form of a *carpe diem* saying, wisdom encourages young folks in the society to get the best out of life (11.9-10). *Lastly,* wisdom issues a call to her audience to live life fully in the *present* and demands that the audience 'remember your Creator' (12.1-7)! To the first audience, the main objective of wisdom's voice interacting with Qohelet's at this strategic juncture is twofold: (1) to affirm the value of wisdom; and (2) to spell out the limits of wisdom in the form of proverbial sayings and poetic pronouncements.

1. Wisdom is indeed better than folly: The strength and limits of wisdom (10.8-20)

⁸ *Whoever digs a pit may fall into it;*
  whoever breaks through a wall may be bitten by a snake.
⁹ *Whoever quarries stones may be injured by them;*
  whoever splits logs may be endangered by them.
¹⁰ *If the axe is dull*
  and its edge unsharpened,
 more strength is needed,
  but skill will bring success.
¹¹ *If a snake bites before it is charmed,*
  the charmer receives no fee.
¹² *Words from the mouth of the wise are gracious,*
  but fools are consumed by their own lips.
¹³ *At the beginning their words are folly;*
  at the end they are wicked madness—
¹⁴   *and fools multiply words.*
 No one knows what is coming—
  who can tell someone else what will happen after them?
¹⁵ *The toil of fools wearies them;*
  they do not know the way to town.
¹⁶ *Woe to the land whose king was a servant*
  and whose princes feast in the morning.
¹⁷ *Blessed is the land whose king is of noble birth*
  and whose princes eat at a proper time—
  for strength and not for drunkenness.

^{18} *Through laziness, the rafters sag;*
  because of idle hands, the house leaks.
^{19} *A feast is made for laughter,*
  wine makes life merry,
  and money is the answer for everything.
^{20} *Do not revile the king even in your thoughts,*
  or curse the rich in your bedroom,
 because a bird in the sky may carry your words,
  and a bird on the wing may report what you say.

Goldingay's comment here provides some directives for our interpretation of 10.8-20. He notes that the two double sayings concern the relationship between 'drive, chance, and smartness' (2021a: 260). Verses 8-10 paint a picture of people's actions that may cause harm to themselves: that is, falling into the pit which one digs; being bitten by a snake after one breaks through a wall; removing stones may injure the quarrier; and being endangered by cutting wood. The interplay between drive–chance–smartness here leaves some space for readers to exercise our imagination. The acts of digging pits, breaking walls, removing stones and splitting logs are not random tasks; they are purposeful. Yet the falling and other harmful results are not merely by chance either. Perhaps, 'smartness/wisdom fails' is the key idea here. These ironies point to the fact that smartness may fail us even when we have given our best efforts, when accidents occur by chance.

Along this interpretive path, vv. 10-11 add another dimension to wisdom's advice. It is a matter of *judgment* (of the wise) to calculate the anticipated outcomes: that is, using a sharpened functional axe to do the job (v. 10) and fulfilling the task of a charmer (v. 11). In the form of two antithetical parallelisms, the beneficial words of the wise (v. 12) are contrasted with the wicked madness of the words of the fools (vv. 13-14). Goldingay suggests that v. 14b may refer to the foolishness of the ruler 'who can't know and can't be told' (2021a: 262). Alternatively, Bartholomew sees that v. 14b gives the affirmation of v. 14a an ironic twist: since 'no one knows what is to come, thus we cannot even be sure that the consequences of folly will eventuate' (2009: 325). Either way, v. 14b is a prelude to v. 15 in its depiction of the problem faced by fools. The toil of fools is wearisome to the extent that they do not know the common way to town (which is expected by everyone).

Wisdom's voice speaks out emphatically in vv. 16-17. Using the formula of the two ways ('blessing and cursing/blessed and woe to'), she presents a contrast between a disastrous ('woe to', v. 16a) government of an immature king who has no idea how to govern (v. 16) and wise governance (v. 17).

The officials of the foolish king feast at the most inappropriate time (in the morning) instead of attending to the business of governance (v. 16b). 'Blessed' is the government whose king is of nobility and knows how to govern. His princes eat at the proper time to nourish themselves for strength to govern instead of merely seeking pleasure in drunkenness (v. 17b). Along the same chain of thought, wisdom cites a traditional maxim: 'Through laziness, the rafters sag; because of idle hands, the house leaks' (v. 18; cf. Prov. 6.6-11; 10.26; 13.4; 15.19; 19.24; 20.4; 26.15). This proverbial saying serves as a metaphor for the results of the officials' self-gratifying leadership (Goldingay 2021a: 267). Bartholomew notes that the depiction of the leaking roof and dripping house is the result of neglect of maintenance due to the laziness of fools. The wise person will take proactive actions toward the maintenance of the house (326).

In the light of 10.6 ('Fools are put in many high positions while the rich occupy the low ones'), where the 'rich' serves as the antithesis of the 'fools', vv. 18-19 here do fit in nicely with the objective of wisdom's speech. Verse 19 addresses the God-approved advice to eat, drink and be merry, as indicated in the *carpe diem* sayings (8.15; 9.7-10). Money is the *answer* to enable one to feast and enjoy life (contra Bartholomew, who sees v. 19 here subverting vv. 16-17; 2009: 326). On the surface, v. 20 seems to be at odds with wisdom's voice. Wisdom warns the audience to watch their speech (not to curse the king or the rich with spoken and unspoken words), as it could be overheard (v. 20b).

Wisdom's sayings in 10.8-20 may seem to be quite randomly grouped together in this polyphony. However, in the context of her twofold objective—(1) affirming that wisdom is indeed more beneficial than folly; and (2) explicating that the superiority of wisdom is found in its capability of exercising 'wise *judgment*' in all situations—wisdom has achieved her objectives. This is amidst the notion of uncertainty that all (the wise and the fools) are facing, and it paves the way for wisdom's voice in 11.1-8, giving advice for life in view of the uncertainties of the risky future.

2. *Advice for life in view of the uncertainties of the risky future (11.1-8)*

11

¹ *Ship your grain across the sea;*
   after many days you may receive a return.
² *Invest in seven ventures, yes, in eight;*
   you do not know what disaster may come upon the land.
³ *If clouds are full of water,*
   they pour rain on the earth.

> *Whether a tree falls to the south or to the north,*
> *in the place where it falls, there it will lie.*
> ⁴ *Whoever watches the wind will not plant;*
> *whoever looks at the clouds will not reap.*
> ⁵ *As you do not know the path of the wind,*
> *or how the body is formed in a mother's womb,*
> *so you cannot understand the work of God,*
> *the Maker of all things.*
> ⁶ *Sow your seed in the morning,*
> *and at evening let your hands not be idle,*
> *for you do not know which will succeed,*
> *whether this or that,*
> *or whether both will do equally well.*
> ⁷ *Light is sweet,*
> *and it pleases the eyes to see the sun.*
> ⁸ *However many years anyone may live,*
> *let them enjoy them all.*
> *But let them remember the days of darkness,*
> *for there will be many.*
> *Everything to come is vanity.*

Wisdom's voice continues to speak out in ch. 11, offering advice for how to live life in view of the uncertainties of the risky future. I see that the overall purpose of wisdom's speech in 11.1-8 is to shape up, to supplement some of the open-ended subjects in Qohelet's reflections (1.12–2.26; 3.16–4.16; 5.13–6.12 [MT 5.12–6.12]; 7.15–10.7) and her own previous pronouncements. Topics such as how to manage the God-given 'lot/portion' and live life fully (cf. 9.7-10) and human incomprehensibility of the work of God (cf. 8.1, 16) are representative examples. Wisdom's speech further expands the benefits of living in contrast to death (see 9.3-6). Moreover, wisdom underscores the notion of the fear of God (see ch. 5) by highlighting that God is the Maker of all things (11.5b).

Two notions are to be employed in shaping our interpretation. *First,* ch. 11 is poetry, and it should be read through such an interpretive lens. Instead of direct statements made by wisdom (e.g. 10.12-15; 9.17-18), there are multiple usages of image and metaphor, and readers are reminded to approach the text with more imagination and openness. *Second,* the strategic position of this wisdom saying between Qohelet's last reflection on his exploration of life (10.5-7) and his last outburst of the motto ('Vanity of vanities! All is vanity!') in 12.8 should be placed in the foreground of interpretation.

In the overall context of the notion that it is good to be alive (Enns 2011: 106), commentators generally agree that the locus of wisdom's speech in 11.1-8 is about 'doing your best while living with the uncertainty and risk of the future (Enns, Bartholomew, Seow, Brown). Brown also underscores the resourcefulness of giving (2007: 101). Focus on the limits of human knowledge in coping with risks as the interpretive drive is found in Enns (2011: 106), Bartholomew (cf. 2009: 335, regarded as the key for interpretation: v. 6b) and Seow (1997: 346). The majority take 11.1-2 as wisdom's encouragement to the first audience to give generously to others and not to expect any good returns (v. 2a). I concur with Lee that the 'giving' in vv. 1-2a is not necessarily a metaphor for foreign investment. It is simply 'a call to charitable deeds . . . without calculating for the potential returns' (2011: 69). Wisdom's voice adds an important dimension: the God-given 'lot' in life. If 'giving generously is about human stewardship, then wisdom is advocating that in the face of all risks in life, one should maintain a good balance between responsibility and catching the opportune time (likewise, cf. Seow 1997: 346). Verses 2b-4, 6a explicate the risks involved as well as the loss of opportunities (no planting and thus no reaping, v. 4b: 'whoever watches the wind will not plant; whoever looks at the clouds will not reap').

In vv. 5-6, wisdom pronounces uncertainty of the future and the unpredictability of what is going to come, and human's inability to understand the work of God who is the Maker of all things (from the cosmic, 'the path of the wind', to the physical realm, 'how the body is formed in a mother's womb', vv. 5a, 6b). Further, in managing our 'lot', wisdom urges diligence and living life to its fullness, using the metaphor of sowing seeds: 'sow your seeds in the morning, and at evening let your hands not be idle' (v. 6b). Toward the end of this section, wisdom's voice turns from an encouraging to a warning tone in vv. 7-8. Employing the imagery of seeing the sun, wisdom paints a picture of the sweetness of light (v. 7). While we can enjoy the light for many years as long as we live, yet 'there will be many days of darkness to come' (v. 8b). With 'light' contrasting 'darkness', wisdom affirms that, on the one hand, light is sweet and to be enjoyed as long as one lives. Yet, on the other hand, days of darkness will come, and will be many (v. 8b). Though humans do not know 'how long they can enjoy the sweetness of light or when and how much the day of darkness will come', one certainty stands firm: the 'sweetness of light' will pass, and the 'days of darkness' will come. Verse 8b presents a sudden twist. In the context of a beautifully crafted poem, wisdom's voice ends with a dire warning: 'But let them remember [for the Hebrew word for "remember", see the discussion in ch. 12] the days of darkness, for there will be many'. Wisdom's voice ends with an outcry, modeling the motto of Qohelet's summary appraisal in chs. 1–10: 'Everything to come is vanity' (v. 8b)!

3. Seventh *carpe diem* saying (11.9-10)

⁹ You who are young, be happy while you are young,
  and let your heart give you joy in the days of your youth.
Follow the ways of your heart
  and whatever your eyes see,
but know that for all these things
  God will bring you into judgment.
¹⁰ So then, banish anxiety from your heart
  and cast off the troubles of your body,
for youth and vigor are vanity.

Reading Ecclesiastes polyphonically, I take 11.9-10 as a continuation of wisdom's voice rather than Qohelet's narration. The reference to 'youth' in this last *carpe diem* saying indicates that as a life stage youth is pertinent. It represents the height of one's vitality, vigour and strength. Wisdom's saying addresses the youth among the first audiences directly: 'You who are young, be happy while you are young' (v. 9). However, on the grounds that 11.8 refers to the whole of one's life, Bartholomew opts for an inclusive addressee among the first audience and sees that the point here is to exhort people to get the foundations of life in place as early as possible (2009: 344). There are debatable interpretive options related to 'follow the ways of your heart and whatever your eyes see' in v. 9a. Lee notes, 'follow the ways of your heart' is an idiom for enjoyment (cf. 5.20 [MT 19]; 6.2; Lee, 74-75). Longman says that the 'heart' and 'eyes' are the 'organs of desire' (1998: 261), and the exhortation here encourages the youth to do whatever their heart desires and not to wait till it is too late. Bartholomew points out that 'following the ways of one's heart' never appears in the other *carpe diem* sayings. The characteristic description in Qohelet's deep reflection— 'I turned/gave my heart' (e.g. 9.1, 11)—indicates that it is Qohelet's 'self' controlling his 'heart', whereas in v. 9, it is the heart that does the leading (2009: 344). It seems quite an ironic encouragement for 'letting your heart cheer you', and 'whatever your eyes see' leads the way. Exercising a reading that is 'cross-graining' (cf. our discussion in the reading strategies section) may yield a multivalent result.

The depth and intensity of Qohelet's reflections are characterized by two expressions: 'I turned/returned and gave my heart . . .' and 'And then I saw . . .'. Both the 'heart' and the eyes' 'vision' (i.e. eyewitness) are the key elements in Qohelet's exploration. There is no irony or contradiction in the interpretation here. Since 'heart' is regarded as both the seat of one's intellect, thought, as well as emotions, 'follow the way of your heart and whatever your eyes see' are both appropriately applied to Qohelet's in-depth and eyewitness reflection of his exploration, as well as vehicles of 'getting joy'. One needs the intuitive 'passion', a *carpe diem* vision, to seek enjoyment because for Ecclesiastes, 'enjoyment is not only permitted, it is commanded; it is not only an opportunity, it is a divine imperative' (Seow 1997: 371). Reading Ecclesiastes as a memoir, the 'giving my heart' and 'seeing' encompass a wealth of emotive investment. I see no disharmony here but the addition of another layer of depth complementarily to the meaning of this *carpe diem* saying (like the production of plywood).

In v. 9c, wisdom's voice makes reference to one certainty: the judgment of God. The young person is reminded that how he rejoices and lives out his life will eventually be accountable to God. To Longman (1998), there is another startling twist in v. 9c that turns positive and upbeat advice into a solemn reminder of the coming judgment. Moreover, wisdom instructs the young person to banish 'anxiety/vexation' from his 'heart' and cast off the 'troubles' from his body (v. 10) and to embrace joy and life in the light of God's coming judgment. Wisdom's voice in v. 10 (also in v. 8) ends with an apparent somber notion: 'For youth and vigor are *hebel* (vanity)!' It is interesting to note that Bartholomew distinctively views that the *hebel* (enigma) in v. 10c has a 'more positive nuance of mystery and points to the limitations of creaturely knowledge' (2009: 345). Given this positive notion, the function of wisdom's voice here is to encourage, to caution and to warn.

4. Live life fully in the 'present' and aware of the certainty of bad times: 'Remember your Creator!' (12.1-7)

12

¹ *Remember your Creator*
   in the days of your youth,
  before the days of trouble come
   and the years approach when you will say,
    'I find no pleasure in them'—
² *before the sun and the light*
   and the moon and the stars grow dark,
   and the clouds return after the rain;
³ *when the keepers of the house tremble,*
   and the strong men stoop,
  when the grinders cease because they are few,
   and those looking through the windows grow dim;

⁴ *when the doors to the street are closed*
  and the sound of grinding fades;
 when people rise up at the sound of birds,
  but all their songs grow faint;
⁵ *when people are afraid of heights*
  and of dangers in the streets;
 when the almond tree blossoms
  and the grasshopper drags itself along
  and desire no longer is stirred.
 Then people go to their eternal home
  and mourners go about the streets.

⁶ *Remember him—before the silver cord is severed,*
  and the golden bowl is broken;
 before the pitcher is shattered at the spring,
  and the wheel broken at the well,
⁷ *and the dust returns to the ground it came from,*
  and the spirit returns to God who gave it.

Two points of entry shape the interpretive strategy of this wisdom discourse: (1) the literary dimension of this poetry; and (2) the significance behind wisdom's call—'Remember your Creator' (v. 1).

Wisdom's voice takes the form of poetry here, elaborating further her thoughts on how to live life fully in the *present*. Lee has insightfully observed that using a series of subordinate clauses with each one introduced by the word 'before' (vv. 1b, 2a, 6a; cf. Lee, 80), wisdom urges the first audience to 'remember/call to mind' the beneficial acts of the Creator God, the Maker of all things (cf. 11.5). The position of the three occurrences of 'before' points to three areas of wisdom's admonition. *First,* 'before' the arrival of bad days (v. 1b)—the 'bad days' are referred to as 'troublesome', 'days when humans will find no pleasure'. The *second* 'before' is in vv. 2-6. This 'call for remembrance' is to be exercised before the unpleasant cosmic phenomena that appear repetitively ('before the sun and the light; and the moon and the stars grow dark' v. 2b); before the impending dangers in life (vv. 3, 5a); before the cessation of all human activities (vv. 3b-4); and before the whole community is faced with calamity (v. 5c). The *third* 'before' points to the disintegration of life, which is depicted in vv. 6-7 ('Before the silver cord is covered, and the golden bowl is broken; before the pitcher is shattered at the spring, and the wheel broken at the well, and the dust returns to the ground it came from, and the spirit returns to God who gave it'). The repetition of the phrase 'before' 'conveys at once the certainty of the deterioration that is to come and the urgency of the *now*' (Lee, 79). Using the rhetoric of a threefold 'before', wisdom's poetic discourse here is an effective means of appealing to the emotions of her first audience—'the youth', building the call for immediate action (act *now*!) up to its climax. Wisdom urges the young to remember God, their Creator, and to live life to its fullness, in the present—*now* 'before' it is too late. The NIV translation adds 'Remember him' to v. 6a ('Remember him—before the silver cord is severed . . .'). Thus v. 1 and vv. 6-7 together form an *inclusio* of wisdom's speech here, highlighting 'remembrance of the Creator' and the need to take immediate action before it is too late—before 'the dust returns to the ground it came from and the spirit returns to God who gave it' (v. 7).

Ecclesiastes 12.1-7 is poetry and is thus open to diverse interpretations of its pictorial description. The depiction covers the cosmic, domestic and economic realms. Loaded with action-oriented and intriguing imagery (e.g. vv. 5b, 5c), it appeals to readers more like an eschatological (end-time) portrayal of all humanity's last days before death. Both Enns and Seow take this as an eschatological poem with specific reference to death (vv. 5b-7; cf. Enns 2009: 108; Seow 1997: 368-69). To think of one's Creator is to think of death, for the life-spirit returns to its giver (12.7). Enns also takes vv. 2-5a as the intervening period between youth and death (108). This line of interpretation will put 'death' (including 'remember your Creator') as the focus of Wisdom's admonition here. In short, wisdom issues an urgent call to the young people to enjoy life in the *present* in the face of death. If the purpose of wisdom's narration is to convey the *urgency (now)*, the target audience are the *young folks*, and the subject matter is to enjoy life in the light of impending *death*, then, as a reader, I find myself in dialectic tension. These notions do not add up to an *admonition* to 'live life fully in the *present*' and to be aware of the certainty of bad times. It would be more in line with a *warning* instead. The significance of 'remember your Creator in the days of your youth' in v. 1 is being undermined.

I take vv. 1, 6, 'Remember your Creator in the days of your youth', as a beautiful inclusion to wisdom's admonition. The Hebrew word for 'remember' (*zakar*) in the Old Testament encompasses three temporal dimensions: past, present and future. It is a key word in the book of Deuteronomy (e.g. 5.15; 8.2, 18; 15.15; 16.12; 24.18, 22) and is used quite frequently in the book of Psalms (9.12; 63.6 [MT 7]; 78.42; 88.5 [MT 6]; 98.3; 106.7; 136.23; 143.5). When it is used with God as the subject, it often refers to God's beneficial acts for God's people, or the covenant. When used with humans as the subject, it signifies that as people remember/recall God's acts of mercy in the *past*, on this experiential basis, the 'act of remembrance' evokes trust and strength for the *present* and hope for the *future* (cf. Deut. 5.15; 8.2, 18; 15.15; 16.12; 24.18, 22 in context). Reading 12.1-7 as wisdom's admonition, we see that she is commending the young people to lay a good foundation early on in life. This is to be done by always calling to mind the Creator God's mercies upon them. This conviction will sustain them through the bad days and carry them through the risky/challenging future till they become old and faced with the inevitable final destiny, death. Yet for the moment, enjoy life and do your best as much as you can in the *present*. If this reading is justified, wisdom is adding on another layer of substance—on living joyfully in the *present* and being aware of the bad days ahead.

K. Qohelet's First-person Summary Appraisal, Echoing the Fundamental Conviction: 'Vanity of Vanities! All Is Vanity!' (12.8)

[8] 'Vanity of vanities!' **SAYS THE PREACHER (QOHELET).**
  'All is vanity!'

After wisdom's voice turns silent, Qohelet's agonizing cry breaks out again at this critical juncture in 12.8. There are three important components to v. 8: (1) Qohelet's 'I'-voice: 'Vanity of vanities!'; (2) the voice of the frame narrator, repositioning Qohelet back to the front stage: 'Says Qohelet/ the preacher'; and (3) Qohelet's 'I'-voice continues: 'All is vanity!' This last outcry is weighty, loaded, a cumulative summary appraisal of all his reflections on his 'personal life experience' (1.12–2.26) and 'exploration in life' (3.16–4.16; 5.13–6.12 [MT 5.12–6.12]; 7.15–10.7). Equally important, it is also his spontaneous response to the voice of wisdom, who just finished speaking (10.8–12.7). This is also the last time that Qohelet's audience hears his voice in the form of an outburst. Occupying a centre stage now, Qohelet is declaring—'Vanity of Vanities! All is Vanity!' In essence, Qohelet is saying, I have not changed a bit the way I look at life through the lenses of my own experience and explorations, with deep reflections (e.g. 'I gave my heart' in 9.1, 11), and after interacting, and counteracting with my pretext—wisdom's authentic voice. I have made earnest attempts to seek wisdom and came to realize both the strength and the limits of wisdom. Yet, I remain persistent in asserting that 'life is utterly absurd! Meaningless!' Human life and its experience under the sun are still a 'mirage'! an 'enigma'! a 'mere breath'! To the audience, after hearing the final *hebel* in 12.8, only a breathtaking, hushed silence lingers (cf. Lee, 79). This paves the way for us to listen to the words of the fifth speaking voice in Ecclesiastes—the epilogist.

L. Voice of the Epilogist Responding to Qohelet's Fundamental Conviction about Life: 'Vanity of Vanities. All Is Vanity!' (12.9-14)

⁹ And more than that[25] the Preacher was wise, but he also imparted knowledge to the people. He pondered and searched out and set in order many proverbs. ¹⁰ The Preacher searched to find just the right words, and what he wrote was upright and true.

¹¹ The words of the wise are like goads, their collected sayings like firmly embedded nails—given by one shepherd. ¹² And more than these,[26] my son, be warned—

Of making many books there is no end, and much study wearies the body.

¹³ Now all has been heard;
   here is the conclusion of the matter:
 Fear God and keep his commandments,
   for this is the duty of all humanity.
¹⁴ For God will bring every deed into judgment,
   including every hidden thing,
   whether it is good or evil.

Qohelet's anguished cry ('Vanity of vanities! All is vanity!') in 1.2 and 12.8 forms a strategic *inclusio* within the book before the epilogist jumps in with the closing remarks (12.9-14). It breaks the dialogic and dialectic thrust of one's reading, leaving the notion of an abrupt and dogmatic statement: 'Fear God and keep his commandments' is required for all humanity (v. 13). It also gives the impression of a quick-fix resolution, most unsatisfying and, to a certain extent, troubling to the reader.

The function of the epilogue in Ecclesiastes has attracted many scholarly interpretations in the recent past (cf. Boda 2013; Sneed 2002; Leung Lai 2021). Through a detailed lexical and thematic study of the epilogue, Andrew Shead noted two framing key words, '*hebel*' and 'fear', which provide a shaping of the dynamics that exist between 12.8-12 and 12.13-14 (1997: 91). The epilogist first legitimizes Qohelet's role as a wise teacher, and he defends the value of wisdom (vv. 9-11). In typical wisdom style (cf. Prov. 1.8; 2.1, etc.), he addresses the audience passionately as 'my son' (v. 12) and attempts to give an apology of the whole book (1.2–12.8) in his concluding remarks. For Qohelet, the pain for the search of wisdom could

---

25. In accordance with the Hebrew text.
26. In accordance with the Hebrew text.

not be resolved through understanding life under the sun. To the epilogist, the wise way is to live in obedient fear of God, who knows and judges all (v. 13). Fox also supports the idea that in an effort to protect Qohelet, the epilogist is combining '*hebel*' and 'fear' to present a composite view of reality: 'Fear God is the right attitude, along with the trust that God is just' (1999: 362). However, for Murphy, reading Ecclesiastes from the perspective of the epilogist as exemplified above is an 'oversimplification' of Qohelet's conflicts as echoed everywhere in his 'I'-voice (1992: lxv).

Ecclesiastes 12.8 represents Qohelet's response to the ideology ingrained in traditional wisdom: 'Fear God and keep his commandments' (v. 13). God's work (v. 14) is beyond our understanding but ultimately is just (see 1.4-7; 2.26; 3.11, 14, 17-18; 6.2; 7.13-14; 8.6-8; 9.1; 11.5-6; 12.1, 7). Qohelet seeks to embrace both—his and the epilogist's—ideologies in all 'flesh' but finds it burdensome and oppressive. The epilogist seeks to defend his ideology by underscoring twice in the epilogue, 'And more than that...' (v. 9) and 'and more than these...' (v. 12), leading to the final statement—'Fear God and keep his commandments for this is the duty of all humankind' (v. 13). Following the suggestion offered by the phrase 'words of the wise' in v. 11, Murphy takes the referent of 'all these' as the wisdom tradition (1992: 125). The final words also bring in the idea that God's just judgment will be upon every deed, good or bad (v. 14).

Throughout the twelve chapters, Qohelet's compelling 'I'-voice is inviting readerly engagement in meaning-making. Toward the conclusion of the book, again, he is encouraging readers to find our own interpretive voice here. As an interpretive option, readers are empowered to read 'against the grain' of the epilogist's oversimplistic way of providing a quick fix to defend the ideology of traditional wisdom ('Here is the conclusion of the matter: Fear God and keep his commandments, for this is the duty of all humankind', v. 13). Or, alternatively, respond 'with the grain' to the epilogist's attempt to 'make it right' in his concluding remarks (12.9-14). Both are possible alternatives for interpretation that are open to us—'the reader'. Most important of all, it is hoped that all interested and engaged readers will come up with a 'reshaped ideology' of your own.

Conclusion

Ecclesiastes is indeed an ambiguous and complex book. In keeping with its characteristic nature, a multi-perspectival approach (reading narratively, reading polyphonically, reading dialectically, reading 'cross the grains', and reading the text as a memoir) has been employed in its interpretation. Throughout this commentary, I have provided pointers and directives along the way. I hope that readers can recognize the 'under the sun' commonality of Qohelet's personal experience and the empirical dimension of Qohelet's explorations. Thus, we all share a slice of the reality in this 'Grand Narrative'. To practise hearing the text, readers can have the firsthand experience of the vibrant dialogic dynamics of the multiplicity of speaking voices and be encouraged to develop our own readerly interpretive voice. Reading dialectically enables us to capture the dialectic tension that occurs everywhere within the twelve chapters and gain a better handling of the contradictions through 'cross-graining'. To be able to get hold of the weighty emotions of the memoirist Qohelet through his compelling 'I'-voice also evokes in us the urge to respond self-engagingly. To a certain extent, these five perspectival readings *together* have yielded a multilayered, enriched outcome for the *polyvalent* meaning-significance of the book.

What, then, is the core message of Ecclesiastes after walking through this multi-perspectival interpretive path? With the empowerment of readers toward meaning-making, I shall deliberately join the multi-voices of this polyphony and offer my interpretive voice here. Ecclesiastes is about the search for the meaning of life and, more specifically, about 'how to live'. Through the captivating 'I'-voice of Qohelet interacting and counteracting with the other voices, I propose here the core message of the book is: 'Embracing coexisting dialectic tensions that are of polar nature is the way to live'. Moreover, it is God's command for us to live life fully in the *present*. Enjoy life with the 'lot' given and approved by God. This God-given 'lot/ portion' must be cultivated and managed with good stewardship. It takes a text with such complex features to bring these messages to the foreground in the broader context of the 'Grand Narrative'. These proposed ideas are truths, but in no way can they represent the whole truth about Ecclesiastes. The interplay of subjectivity, polyvalence and indeterminacy still plays an important role as it explicates the dynamics of our own meaning-making

Conclusion

(encouraged all along this interpretive path as the sixth voice in the process of reading).

Ecclesiastes underlines a paradigm of 'how to live', and it is rooted in the commonality of the 'collective lived experience of all humanity under the sun'. If the nature of the book is paradoxical, then, let it remain a 'paradox'. In the context of 'lived experience under the sun', conflicting ideologies, layers of dialectic tension, laments for the nonsensicality and absurdity of life along with encouragement to enjoy life with all its pleasures—these features are all within the normality of the realities of human life. Timothy Walton's insightful comment may call for some re-orientation for our readers. He states, readers 'can allow the truth of both (conflicting) perspectives to remain side by side and confess that a resolution to how these can both be true escapes us, even the wisest among us' (cf. 8.17; 2011:130; word in parentheses mine).

This book is dedicated to the memory of my peers—those among the cloud of witnesses. '*Remember* your Creator' (12.1, 6) is one of wisdom's admonitions in the book. As I *remember* God's gracious acts: *past, present, future,* I can continue journeying strong while seeking to embrace the coexisting dialectic tensions. Yet, amidst the harshness of life, there are still glimpses of uplifting momentum (*carpe diem*) and exultant joy in life.

Select Bibliography

Commentaries

Bartholomew, Craig G.
   2009   *Ecclesiastes* (BCOTWP; Grand Rapids, MI: Baker Academic).
Brown, William P.
   2000   *Ecclesiastes* (Interpretation; Louisville, KY: John Knox Press).
Christianson, Eric S.
   2007   *Ecclesiastes through the Centuries* (Blackwell Bible Commentaries; Malden, MA: Blackwell Publishing).
Crenshaw, J.L.
   1987   *Ecclesiastes: A Commentary* (OTL; Philadelphia: Westminster).
Enns, Peter
   2011   *Ecclesiastes* (Two Horizons Old Testament Commentary; Grand Rapids, MI: Eerdmans).
Fox, Michael V.
   1999   *A Time to Tear Down and a Time to Build: A Rereading of Ecclesiastes* (Grand Rapids, MI: Eerdmans).
   2004   *Ecclesiastes: The Traditional Hebrew Text with the New JPS Translation* (Philadelphia: Jewish Publication Society).
Goldingay, John
   2021a *Ecclesiastes* (The Bible in God's World; Eugene, OR: Cascade Books).
Heim, Knut
   2019   *Ecclesiastes* (TOTC, 18; Downers Grove, IL: InterVarsity Press).
Krüger, Thomas
   2004   *Qoheleth* (ed. Klaus Baltzer; trans. O.C. Dean Jr.; Hermeneia; Minneapolis, MN: Fortress Press).
Longman, Tremper, III
   1998   *The Book of Ecclesiastes* (NICOT; Grand Rapids, MI: Eerdmans).
Murphy, Roland E.
   1992   *Ecclesiastes* (WBC, 23A; Waco, TX: Word).
Seow, Choon-Leong
   1997   *Ecclesiastes* (AB; New York: Doubleday).
Weeks, Stuart
   2020   *Ecclesiastes 1–5: A Critical and Exegetical Commentary* (ICC; 2 vols.; London: T. & T. Clark [Bloomsbury Publishing]).
   2021   *Ecclesiastes 5–12: A Critical and Exegetical Commentary* (ICC; 2 vols.; London: T. & T. Clark [Bloomsbury Publishing]).
Whybray, R.N.
   1989   *Ecclesiastes* (NCB; Grand Rapids, MI: Eerdmans).

Special Studies and Articles on Ecclesiastes

Bartholomew, C.G.
    1998   *Reading Ecclesiastes: Old Testament Exegesis and Hermeneutical Theory* (Analecta Biblica, 139; Rome: Pontifical Biblical Institute Press).

Boda, Mark
    2013   'Speaking into the Silence: The Epilogue of Ecclesiastes', in Mark J. Boda et al. (eds.), *The Word of the Wise Are Like Goads: Engaging Qohelet in the 21st Century* (Winona Lake, IN: Eisenbraus): 257-82.

Christianson, Eric S.
    1998   *A Time to Tell: Narrative Strategies in Ecclesiastes* (JSOTSup, 280; Sheffield: Sheffield Academic Press).

Fox, Michael V.
    1997   'Frame-Narrative and Composition in the Book of Qohelet', *Hebrew Union College Annual* 48: 83-106.

Greenwood, Kyle R.
    2012   'Debating Wisdom: The Role of Voice in Ecclesiastes', *CBQ* 74: 476-91.

Jarick, J.
    2014   'Ecclesiastes among the Comedians', in K.J. Dell and W. Kynes (eds.), *Reading Ecclesiastes Intertextually* (London: Bloomsbury T. & T. Clark): 176-88.

Lee, Eunny P.
    2005   *The Vitality of Enjoyment in Qohelet's Theological Rhetoric* (New York: de Gruyter).

Leung Lai, Barbara M.
    2013   'Voice and Ideology in Ecclesiastes: Reading "Cross the Grain"', in James K. Aitken, Jeremy M.C. Clines and Christl M. Maier (eds.), *Interested Readers: Essays on the Hebrew Bible in Honor of David J.A. Clines* (Atlanta, GA: Society of Biblical Literature): 265-78.
    2014   'The Preacher and One's Own "Text-of-Life"', in Mark Roncace and Joseph Weaver (eds.), *Global Perspectives on the Old Testament* (Upper Saddle River, NJ: Pearson): 214-17.
    2019a   'Engaging Ecclesiastes Narratively and Polyphonically with a Chinese Lens: Traditional Wisdom and "Collective Lived Experience under the Sun" in Dialogue', in Uriah Y. Kim and Seung Ai Yang (eds.), *T & T Clark Handbook of Asian American Biblical Hermeneutics* (London: T. & T. Clark): 306-16.
    2019b   'Toward a Version of "Narratival Hermeneutics"—Reading Ecclesiastes Ethnoculturally with a Chinese Lens: Selfhood, Diaspora Experience, and the Search for Meaning', in Néstor Medina, Alison Hari-Singh and Hyeran Kim-Cragg (eds.), *Reading in Between: How Minoritized Cultural Communities Interpret the Bible in Canada* (Eugene, OR: Pickwick Publications): 36-51.
    2021   'Making Some Sense of the Paradox: Polyphony, Conflicting Ideologies, Dialogism, and the Dialectic Dynamics of Ecclesiastes', *OTE* 34: 902-14.

Ryken, Philip Graham
    2010   *Ecclesiastes: Why Everything Matters* (Preaching the Word; Wheaton, IL: Crossway).

Shead, Andrew G.
    1997   'Reading Ecclesiastes Epilogically', *TynB* 50: 67-91.
Sneed, Mark
    2002   '(Dis)closure in Qohelet: Qohelet Deconstructed', *JSOT* 27: 115-26.
Sun, Chloe
    2017   'Ecclesiastes among the Megilloth: Death as the Interthematic Link', *BBR* 27: 185-206.
Walton, Timothy
    2006   *Experimenting with Qohelet: A Text-Linguistic Approach to Reading Qohelet as Discourse* (Amsterdamse Cahiers voorall Exegese van Bijbel en zijn Tradities, Supplement series, 5; Maastricht: Shaker Publishing).
    2011   'Reading Qoheleth as Text, Author, and Readers', in W.T. Van Peursen and J.W. Dyk (eds.), *Tradition and Innovation in Biblical Interpretation: Studies Presented to Professor Eep Talstra on the Occasion of his Sixty-fifth Birthday* (Leiden: Brill): 113-31.
Weeks, Stuart
    2012   *Ecclesiastes and Skepticism* (London: T. & T. Clark).

Other Reference Works

Alonso Schökel, L.
    1998   *A Manual of Hebrew Poetics* (Rome: Editrice Pontifico Istituto Biblico).
Bakhtin, Mikhael M.
    1984   *Problem of Dostoevsky's Poetics* (ed. and trans. Caryl Emerson; Minneapolis: University of Minnesota Press).
    1986a   *The Dialogic Imagination: Four Essays* (ed. Michael Holquist; trans. Caryl Emerson and Michael Holquist; Austin: University of Texas Press).
    1986b   'The Problem of Speech Genre', in *Speech Genre and Other Late Essays* (trans. V. McGee; Austin: University of Texas Press).
Berlin, Adele
    1994   *Poetics and Interpretation of Biblical Narrative* (Winona Lake, IN: Eisenbrauns, 1994).
Culp, A.J.
    2019   *Memoir of Moses: The Literary Creation of Covenantal Memory in Deuteronomy* (Minneapolis, MN: Fortress Press).
Deasey, Louisa
    2018   https://louisadeasey.com/2018/10/10/thebasics-of-memoir.
Fetzer, Anita, and Etsuko Oishi (eds.)
    2011   *Context and Contexts* (Amsterdam: John Benjamins Publishing).
Goldingay, John
    2009   *Old Testament Theology: Israel's Life,* vol. 3 (3 vols.; Downers Grove, IL: IVP).
    2021b   *The Book of Jeremiah* (NICOT; Grand Rapids, MI: Eerdmans).
Kessler, John
    2013   *Old Testament Theology: Divine Call and Human Response* (Waco, TX: Baylor University Press).

Landy, Francis
 2000 'Vision and Voice in Isaiah', *JSOT* 88: 19-36.
 2004 'The Personal Voice in First-Person Narrative Fiction', *Narrative* 12: 113-51.
Larson, Thomas
 2007 *The Memoir and the Memoirist: Reading and Writing Personal Narrative* (Athens, OH: Swallow Press/Ohio University Press).
Leung Lai, Barbara M.
 2011 *Through the 'I'-Window: The Inner Life of Characters in the Hebrew Bible* (HBM, 35; Sheffield: Sheffield-Phoenix Press).
 2015 '"I"-Voice, Emotion, and Selfhood in Nehemiah', *OTE* 28.1: 154-67.
Maguire, Mary H.
 2006 'Autoethnography: Answerability/Responsibility in Authoring Self and Others in the Social Sciences/Humanities', *FQS* 7.2: Article 16.
Medina, Néstor, Alison Hari-Singh and Hyeran Kim-Cragg (eds.)
 2019 *Reading in Between: How Minoritized Cultural Communities Interpret the Bible in Canada* (Eugene, OR: Pickwick Publications).
Newsom, Carol A.
 1996 'Bakhtin, the Bible, and Dialogic Truth', *JR* 76: 290-306.
 2002 'The Book of Job as a Polyphonic Text', *JSOT* 97: 87-108.
 2009 'Reflection on Ideological Criticism and Postcritical Perspectives', in Joel M. Leon and Kent Harold Richards (eds.), *Method Matters: Essays in the Interpretation of the Hebrew Bible in Honor of David Patterson* (Atlanta, GA: Society of Biblical Literature): 553-57.
North, R.
 1993 'Brain and Nerve in the Biblical Outlook', *Bib* 74: 592-97.
Osborne, Grant R.
 1991 *The Hermeneutical Spiral* (Downers Grove, IL: IVP).
Petersen, David L., and Kent H. Richards
 1992 *Interpreting Hebrew Poetry* (GBS; Minneapolis, MN: Fortress Press).
Perdue, Leo G.
 1994 *Wisdom and Creation: The Theology of Wisdom Literature* (Nashville, TN: Abingdon).
Snodgrass, Klyne
 2002 'Reading to Hear: A Hermeneutics of Hearing', *HBT* 24: 1-32.
Smith, Mark S.
 1998 'The Heart and Innards in Israelite Emotional Expressions: Notes from Anthropology and Psychology', *JBL* 117: 427-36.
Steck, O.H.
 2000 *The Prophetic Books and the Theological Witness* (trans. J.D. Nogalski; St. Louis, MO: Chalice Press).
Sternberg, Meir
 1985 *The Poetics of Biblical Narrative* (Bloomington: Indiana University Press).
 1986 'The World from the Addressee's Viewpoint: Reception as Representation, Dialogue as Monologue', *Style* 20: 295-318.
Thienhaus, Ole J.
 1999 'Jewish Time: Ancient Practice, Hellenistic and Modern Habits, Freud's Reclaiming Judaism', *American Jewish Congress* 48: 440-45.

Yorke, Gosnell L.
   1999   'Visible but Voiceless Minorities No More: New Readings of the Bible in Canada', in Néstor Media, Alison Hari-Singh and Hyeran Kim-Cragg (eds.), *Reading in Between: How Minoritized Cultural Communities Interpret the Bible in Canada* (Eugene, OR: Pickwick Publications): 112-21.

Index of References

HEBREW BIBLE/		Judges		78.42	104
OLD TESTAMENT		9.16	54	88.5	104
		14.18	88	88.6	104
Genesis				98.3	104
1–11	87	1 Samuel		104.15	90
3.19	87	17.43	88	106.7	104
4.1	53			135.14	69
6.5	87	2 Samuel		136.23	104
26.29	54	19.9	69	143.5	104
35.19-20	68			147.3	86
35.28-29	68	Job			
		9.25	47	Proverbs	
Numbers		21.17	42	1.4	98
23.24	88	28–29	42	1.7	62, 63, 73
				1.8	106
Deuteronomy		Psalms		2.1	106
1.15	76	1	84	3.2	83
3.14-15	76	1.1-4	1	3.13-17	83
5.6	76	4.7	86	3.33	1, 42, 51, 75,
5.7	76	4.8	86		76, 83, 84
5.15	104, 105	9.1	86	4.18-19	49
6.18	54	9.2	86	5	78
7.13-14	76	9.12	104	6.6-11	98
7.15-18	76	13.2	86	7	78
7.18	76	13.3	86	10.26	98
8.2	104, 105	13.5	86	10.27	83
8.18	104, 105	13.6	86	15.19	98
11.26-28	1, 51, 75, 76,	16.5-6	57	19.24	98
	83, 84	16.9	86	20.4	98
15.15	104, 105	34.8	47	24.21	81
16.12	104, 105	34.9	47	25.6	81
24.18	104, 105	34.18	86	26.15	98
24.22	104, 105	34.19	86		
28	76	44	84	Ecclesiastes	
28.1	1, 75	51.16	86	1–12	16
28.15	1, 75	51.17	86	1–10	101
		63.6	104	1	9, 16, 40
Joshua		63.7	104	1.1-21	4
24.29-30	68	73	84	1.1-11	36

Ecclesiastes (cont.)		2.1	1, 8, 10, 38, 46, 47	3.2	56
1.1-3	38, 40			3.3	53
1.1-2	1, 3, 9, 10, 40	2.2	47	3.4	53
1.1	2, 3, 9, 37, 40	2.3-14	9	3.6	53, 91
1.2–6.9	36	2.3	47, 63	3.8	53, 86
1.2-13	17	2.4-11	47	3.9	53, 54, 57
1.2-3	37	2.4-9	14	3.10-11	11
1.2	1, 2, 14, 37, 41, 106	2.7-8	47	3.10	20, 54
		2.9-15	58	3.11	53, 54, 91, 107
1.3–3.15	56	2.9	47		
1.3-11	9	2.10	47, 57	3.12-15	54
1.3	41, 42, 53, 54	2.11-25	19	3.12-14	55, 63
1.4-11	5, 38, 41-43	2.11	38, 46, 47	3.12-13	1, 11, 38, 53, 54
1.4-8	41	2.12-26	8		
1.4-7	42, 107	2.12-23	38, 47, 51	3.12	53
1.4	43	2.12-16	48	3.13-14	63
1.5	42, 43	2.12-13	47	3.13	47, 57
1.6	42, 43	2.12	4, 14, 48, 49	3.14-15	11, 38, 54, 63, 81
1.7	42, 43	2.13	48, 63		
1.8-11	42, 43	2.14-23	48	3.14	53, 54, 107
1.8	42-44	2.14	49	3.15	53, 55
1.9-11	42, 43, 55	2.15	4, 9, 10, 14, 47-49, 52	3.16–4.16	3, 4, 13, 38, 55, 99, 105
1.9-10	43				
1.9	43, 53	2.16	49	3.16-22	8
1.10	4, 42-44	2.17-26	48	3.16-21	38, 55
1.11	43, 44	2.17-25	49	3.16-17	11
1.12–12.8	36	2.17-19	12	3.16	56
1.12–2.26	3, 4, 13, 38, 41, 44, 50, 99, 105	2.17-18	11, 49	3.17-22	21
		2.17	38, 47-49, 52, 58	3.17-18	1, 56, 107
				3.17	9, 56
1.12–2.16	2	2.18-21	57	3.18-20	56
1.12-18	38, 44	2.19	48, 49, 52	3.18	8
1.12-17	44	2.21	48, 49, 52	3.19	56
1.12-15	9	2.22	48, 49	3.21-22	4
1.12-14	1	2.23	38, 47-49, 52	3.21	56
1.12	2, 45	2.24-26	38, 50, 63	3.22	1, 11, 14, 38, 56, 57
1.13	45	2.24-25	1, 11		
1.14-18	8, 18	2.24	47, 51, 57	4	21, 57
1.14	1, 38, 44, 45	2.25	4, 51	4.1-4	9
1.15	10, 45	2.26	1, 11, 20, 38, 47, 48, 50-52, 107	4.1-3	3, 8, 12, 21, 38, 57
1.16	1, 8-10, 14, 45				
				4.1	5, 8, 58
1.17-18	9	3	20, 52	4.2	58
1.17	38, 44, 45	3.1-16	20	4.3	58
1.18	45, 46	3.1-15	38, 52, 56	4.4-16	22
2	18, 52	3.1-11	38, 52, 81	4.4-6	8, 12
2.1-11	8, 38, 46	3.1-8	5, 9, 81	4.4	14, 38, 58
2.1-10	18	3.1	52, 53	4.5-6	9, 38, 58
2.1-2	1, 9, 10, 14	3.2-8	52, 53	4.5-3	4

4.7-16	38, 59	5.9-11	64	6.9-12	69	
4.7-12	12	5.9	63, 64	6.9	68, 69	
4.7-10	8	5.10-12	64	6.10–8.17	36	
4.7-8	60	5.11	66	6.10-12	69	
4.7	8, 14, 21, 57	5.12–6.12	39, 64, 99, 105	6.10	69	
4.8	59, 60			6.11	68, 69	
4.9-14	4, 9, 38, 59, 60	5.12-19	8	6.12	68, 69	
		5.12-16	3, 24, 39, 64-67	7	9, 25, 65, 70	
4.9-13	1, 9			7.1-14	39, 70	
4.9	59, 60	5.12-13	65	7.1-12	39, 70	
4.10-14	60	5.12	4, 13, 14, 65, 66	7.1-10	25	
4.10	60			7.1-5	10	
4.11-12	8	5.13–6.12	39, 64, 99, 105	7.1	71	
4.11	60			7.2	71, 72	
4.12	60	5.13–6.9	68	7.3	71, 72	
4.13-14	60, 61, 63	5.13-20	8	7.4	71, 72	
4.13	60, 81	5.13-17	3, 24, 39, 64-67	7.5	71	
4.14-16	22, 61			7.6	71-73	
4.15-16	8, 38, 59, 60	5.13-14	65	7.7-12	75	
4.15	14, 61	5.13	4, 13, 14, 65, 66	7.7	3, 71-73	
4.16	1, 61			7.8	71, 72	
4.17–5.19	61	5.14-16	67	7.9	73	
4.17–5.7	63	5.15-20	24	7.10	71, 73	
4.17–5.6	2, 4, 39, 61-63, 81	5.15-17	67	7.11-22	26	
		5.15	65	7.11-12	73	
4.17	62, 86	5.16	65, 66	7.11	73	
5	23, 61, 63, 99	5.17-19	1, 11, 39, 66, 67	7.12-13	39	
5.1–6.9	36			7.12	13, 73, 83	
5.1-20	61	5.17	8, 57, 66	7.13-14	73, 74, 86, 107	
5.1-14	23	5.18-20	1, 11, 39, 66, 67			
5.1-8	63			7.14	74, 91	
5.1-7	1, 4, 39, 61-63, 81	5.18	8, 57, 66, 67	7.15–10.7	3, 4, 13, 39, 74, 99, 105	
		5.19	66, 67			
5.1-2	62	5.20	66, 101	7.15-28	10	
5.1	4, 61, 62, 86	6	24, 70	7.15-18	8, 39, 74, 77	
5.2-7	62	6.1-12	8, 39, 67-70	7.15-16	74	
5.2-3	62	6.1-7	24	7.15	1, 5, 10-12, 14, 49, 73, 75	
5.2	4, 62	6.1-6	3			
5.3-4	86	6.1-2	68	7.16-17	75	
5.3	62	6.1	5, 68	7.16	75	
5.4-5	86	6.2-9	68	7.17-18	75	
5.6	62	6.2	68, 101, 107	7.17	75	
5.7–6.9	36	6.3-9	68	7.18	11	
5.7-11	39, 61, 63	6.3-6	68, 69	7.19-22	39, 74, 77	
5.7-8	3	6.6	4, 68, 69	7.19	77	
5.7	62-64	6.7-12	68	7.20	77	
5.8-12	39, 61, 63	6.7	68	7.21	77	
5.8-9	3	6.8-12	25	7.22	77	
5.8	63, 64	6.8	68, 69	7.23-29	27	

Ecclesiastes (cont.)		8.14	5, 10, 12, 14,	10.1	10, 93		
7.23-26	39, 77, 78		39, 49, 83, 84	10.2	94		
7.23-25	77	8.15	1, 11, 39, 57,	10.4	94		
7.23-24	12, 78		84, 98	10.5-15	8		
7.23	78	8.16-17	39, 85, 86	10.5-7	12, 39, 58,		
7.24-28	91	8.16	8, 10, 14, 82,		94, 99		
7.24	78		85, 99	10.5	10, 14, 94		
7.25-29	8	8.17	14, 85, 86,	10.6	94, 98		
7.25	78, 79, 83		91, 109	10.7	56, 94, 95		
7.26-29	79, 81	9	28, 85	10.8–12.7	39, 95		
7.26	78	9.1–12.8	36	10.8-20	31, 39, 95-98		
7.27–8.8	39, 79	9.1-10	8	10.8-17	96		
7.27-29	79, 80	9.1-6	1, 88	10.8-10	97		
7.27	1, 2, 9, 10,	9.1-2	28, 39, 85-88	10.8	95		
	79	9.1	11, 14, 86-88,	10.10-11	97		
7.28	79		101, 105, 107	10.10	97		
7.29	11, 79, 83	9.2-3	87, 88	10.11	97		
8	27	9.2	86	10.12-15	99		
8.1-8	39, 79-81, 83	9.3-11	29	10.12	97		
8.1-5	27	9.3-6	39, 87, 88, 99	10.13-14	97		
8.1	80-82, 99	9.3	87, 88	10.14	97		
8.2-9	3	9.4-6	87, 88	10.15	97		
8.2-8	81	9.5-6	88	10.16-17	97, 98		
8.2-5	81	9.5	88	10.16	97, 98		
8.2-4	82	9.7–10.4	92	10.17	97, 98		
8.2	81	9.7-10	1, 11, 39, 88-	10.18-20	97		
8.3	81		91, 98, 99	10.18-19	98		
8.4	81	9.7-9	89	10.18	98		
8.5-8	82	9.7	89	10.19	98		
8.5-6	81	9.8	89	10.20	3, 98		
8.5	81	9.9	47, 90	11	31, 99		
8.6-17	28	9.10	79, 88, 90, 91	11.1-8	39, 96, 98-		
8.6-8	107	9.11-12	8, 39, 91		100		
8.6	81	9.11	91, 92, 101,	11.1-3	31, 98		
8.7-8	81		105	11.1-2	100		
8.7	81	9.12-18	30	11.1	90, 95		
8.9-14	84	9.13-18	8	11.2-5	95		
8.9-13	39, 82	9.13-16	39, 92, 93	11.2-4	100		
8.9	82, 83	9.13	4, 92	11.2	100		
8.10-12	8, 83	9.14-15	92	11.3-10	32		
8.10	83	9.14	92	11.4-8	99		
8.11-13	11	9.16	92	11.4	100		
8.11	83	9.17–10.25	93	11.5-6	100, 107		
8.12-14	11, 84	9.17–10.4	39, 93	11.5	99, 100, 103		
8.12-13	39, 82, 83	9.17-18	99	11.6	95, 100		
8.12	10, 83	9.17	93	11.7-8	100		
8.13	83	9.18	93	11.8	100-102		
8.14-17	8	10	30	11.9-10	1, 11, 39, 95,		
8.14-15	1	10.1-7	30		96, 101		

11.9	101, 102	12.6	103, 104, 109	*Isaiah*		
11.10	102	12.7	104, 107	61.1	86	
12	9, 32, 100, 102	12.8-12	106			
		12.8	1-3, 9-12, 14, 40, 95, 99, 105-107	*Jeremiah*		
12.1-7	39, 96, 102, 104, 105			4.19	86	
				5.28	69	
12.1-3	32, 102	12.9-14	2, 9, 10, 12, 14, 36, 37, 40, 95, 106, 107	30.13	69	
12.1	103, 104, 107, 109			*Hosea*		
12.2-6	103			11.3	53	
12.2-5	104	12.9-11	106	11.8	86	
12.2	103	12.9	2, 11, 107			
12.3-4	103	12.10	2	*Malachi*		
12.3	103	12.11	107	1.2-3	86	
12.4-13	33	12.12	11, 106, 107			
12.4-7	103	12.13-14	106			
12.5-7	104	12.13	10, 107			
12.5	103, 104	12.14	34, 95, 107			
12.6-7	103, 104					

Index of Authors

Alonso Schökel, L.   10, 45

Bakhtin, M.M.   9
Bartholomew, C.G.   5, 53, 62, 72, 95, 97, 98, 100-102
Berlin, A.   45
Boda, M.   50, 106
Brown, W.P.   50, 66, 73, 86, 100

Crenshaw, J.L.   36, 50, 53, 82, 95
Culp, A.J.   13

Deasey, L.   14

Enns, P.   6, 36, 53, 62, 68, 69, 73, 78, 80, 90, 92, 93, 95, 100, 104

Fetzer, A.   7
Fox, M.V.   2, 5, 10, 41, 49-51, 53, 55, 77, 78, 80-82, 84, 90, 94, 107

Goldingay, J.   3, 4, 6, 37, 40, 42, 49, 54, 63, 68, 72, 75, 84, 86, 88, 89, 95, 97, 98
Greenwood, K.R.   1, 8

Hari-Singh, A.   7
Heim, K.   2, 3, 5, 6, 37, 53, 63-65, 68, 75, 78, 81, 87-90, 93, 95

Jarick, J.   2, 64

Kessler, J.   4, 50
Kim-Cragg, H.   7
Krüger, T.   3, 37, 40, 41, 63, 87, 90, 93, 94

Landy, F.   8, 9
Larson, T.   13

Lee, E.P.   51, 54, 55, 57, 84, 85, 89-91, 100, 101, 103-105
Leung Lai, B.M.   1, 7-9, 12, 13, 58, 106
Longman, T., III   2, 6, 36, 54, 78, 79, 101, 102

Maguire, M.H.   13
Medina, N.   7
Murphy, R.E.   22, 28, 36, 47, 61, 73, 82, 83, 95, 107

Newsom, C.A.   9, 11, 12
North, R.   45

Oishi, E.   7
Osborne, G.R.   35

Perdue, L.G.   5
Petersen, D.L.   43

Richards, K.H.   43
Ryken, P.G.   68

Seow, C.-L.   3, 36, 55, 78, 79, 95, 100, 102, 104
Shead, A.G.   106
Smith, M.S.   86
Sneed, M.   106
Snodgrass, K.   9
Steck, O.H.   35
Sternberg, M.   10, 45
Sun, C.   56, 88

Thienhaus, O.J.   52

Walton, T.   36, 109
Weeks, S.   36, 65, 73, 95
Whybray, R.N.   50

Yorke, G.L.   7

www.ingramcontent.com/pod-product-compliance
Lightning Source LLC
Chambersburg PA
CBHW070335230426
43663CB00011B/2329